SHIPS IN FOCUS
New Zealand and Federal Lines

John Clarkson   Roy Fenton

SURREY (2) *1919; see page 27*

Front cover: **RANGITANE (1)** *1929; see page 36*

Published 1995 by John and Marion Clarkson, 18 Franklands,
Longton, Preston PR4 5PD, United Kingdom.
Reprinted 1997
© 1995 John Clarkson and Roy Fenton

Typeset from disk by Highlight Type Bureau Ltd., Bradford.
Printed by Amadeus Press Ltd., Huddersfield.

ISBN 0 9521179 7 5 [hardback]

FOREWORD

Reactions to *Ships in Focus* have been overwhelmingly favourable, and even those who have written to us with minor comments have been complementary. However, as one reader seems to have misunderstood the scope of our last book, we would like to take this opportunity to set out the philosophy behind the series.

It has never been our intention to feature every ship in a given fleet. In most cases, this would simply not be possible, as photographs do not seem to exist of many ships whose careers ended before or during the first world war, or which had very short lives. In some cases photographs are available but are not of an acceptable standard. What we have done is to show how a fleet developed by including photographs of representative ships from all periods of its history. Where necessary, we have gone to other photographers and collections to make this representation as complete as possible. Inevitably, photographic coverage of modern ships is good, and recognising that these are the ones which will be remembered by most of our readers, we have indulged ourselves by including shots of whole classes, and occasional ships in subsequent owner's colours. The captions to the photographs put a ship or class into its historical context and include the details likely to be of interest to the enthusiast: date and builder, gross tonnage, length, date leaving the fleet, any subsequent names, and ultimate fate. In producing *Ships in Focus* we have three goals: good representation of the fleet, the best possible standard of reproduction, and a high degree of accuracy.

In this, the third *Ships in Focus* book, we illustrate the development of the fleets of the New Zealand Shipping Co. Ltd. and Federal Steam Navigation Co. Ltd. As these companies were in common ownership from 1912, there has been a considerable interchange of ships and many later classes were spread across the two fleets. The ships therefore appear in approximate chronological order, with related New Zealand and Federal ships grouped together. Also included are representative ships of the subsidiary, Avenue Shipping Co. Ltd.

Notwithstanding the comments in the second paragraph, we have found that the New Zealand and Federal fleets have been particularly well photographed, no doubt because of the interest in these ships in Australasia. This means we have found good quality shots of the majority of the companies' steamers and motorships, including every ship owned since 1918. We have therefore increased the number of pages in this volume from 72 to 88 to include more pictures.

To achieve such a wide coverage, photographs from John's collection have been supplemented from elsewhere and, once again, we extend our grateful thanks to everyone who has helped.

John Clarkson, Longton
Roy Fenton, Wimbledon
September 1995

TEKOA (3) *of 1966 in P. & O. colours; see page 78*

NEW ZEALAND AND FEDERAL LINES: SHIPS TO MATCH THE SOUTHERN OCEAN

New Zealand Shipping Co. Ltd. and the Federal Steam Navigation Co. Ltd. have a special place in the pantheon of British cargo liner companies. Their ships operated on the world's longest blue water service and, as if to show their disdain for the oceans, had a powerful even haughty appearance. This was not just show, for the companies' steamers and motorships had an excellent record of withstanding stress of weather.

As its name implies, the New Zealand Shipping Co. Ltd. was originally locally-owned, the company being registered in Christchurch during January 1873. It was launched in competition with Shaw, Savill and Co., who responded with a freight war, although in the nature of these things agreement was eventually reached and the erstwhile rivals became conference partners. However, the competition did force Shaw, Savill to merge with the Albion Line.

Initially the company owned and chartered only sailing vessels. Its 18-strong fleet of iron ships and barques, with their black-and-white painted ports, became something of an institution. It was not unusual for them to sight no land during a passage of at least three months between the United Kingdom and New Zealand. Any emigrant prepared to undergo such a journey, even with free or assisted passages, must have been made of stern stuff, but the New Zealand government hankered after "a better class of immigrant." They pressured the company to employ steam ships, even though experiments from 1879 onwards showed that with existing marine engine technology such long-distance services could not be made to pay. Nevertheless, fear that the government might otherwise start its own service and demands from shippers for refrigerated capacity led the New Zealand Shipping Co. Ltd. to increase its capital in 1882 as a preliminary to ordering five large steamers to carry passengers and frozen meat. Late in 1883 these steamers started to take over services which had been begun earlier that year by chartered tonnage. During each passage no less than three calls were made for bunkers, but even then the steamers' appetite for coal meant that cargo capacity and earnings were seriously restricted by the large bunkers required.

A monthly steamer service between the United Kingdom and New Zealand was viable only with a government mail subsidy, and when this was withdrawn during a trade depression the company ran into problems. The rescuer, or perhaps the predator, was British shipping financier Sir Edwyn Dawes, who was closely associated with the British India S.N. Co. Ltd., P. & O. and several Australian companies. His acquisition of a substantial shareholding meant that in 1890 control of the company passed from New Zealand to London, where it remained. Dawes quickly began replacing the original steamers with more economical vessels, taking advantage of rapid advances in marine engineering such as the development of quadruple expansion engines. He also ensured the disposal of the company's remaining sailing ships. Despite the ending of sail, the company persisted in its practice of flying above its houseflag a steam cornet - a red, white and blue pennant originally meant to distinguish its steam ships from its sailing vessels.

The New Zealand Shipping Co. Ltd. grew in strength over the next 20 years, but in 1912 it was merged, at least financially, with the Federal Steam Navigation Co. Ltd. owned by Birt, Potter and Hughes Ltd. There is some disagreement about who took over whom, but conclusions can be drawn from the observation that Federal's boss Allan Hughes eventually succeeded to the overall chairmanship. The fleets retained their identities, but were managed as one concern.

Federal first appeared in 1895, initially in the Australian trade but adding a New Zealand service in 1902. The company could claim a tenuous connection with Money Wigram and Co. and their celebrated Blackwall frigates; one of the links being their houseflag, which was also carried on the steamers' dark red funnels. The story goes that Money Wigram's SIR EDWARD PAGET was anchored at Spithead flying a white flag carrying a red St. George's cross. The Royal Navy insisted that only a ship with an admiral aboard could fly such a flag, and SIR EDWARD PAGET was ordered to take it down. Her master, thumbing his nose at the Navy, had a blue patch sewn on the centre of the flag and hoisted it once again. This became the houseflag of the owners, and its inheritance by Federal ensured its survival for over a century and a half.

In 1916 the New Zealand and Federal companies were acquired by P. & O. Steam Navigation Co., although their management was to remain independent for half a century. This transaction was but one of a number which saw previously independent British liner companies passing into the control of a small number of powerful financiers. It was ironic that the inflated valuation of the larger companies which helped make this possible, and made many shareholders seriously rich, was a result of the heavy losses of ships and their crews through commerce raiding by German submarines and surface ships. The individual ship's histories in this book will show that New Zealand and Federal ships and seagoing personnel shared fully in this sacrifice.

From an external viewpoint these major changes in ownership become apparent only gradually. A few ships, such as Federal's SHROPSHIRE, were transferred between the companies to cover gaps caused by war losses. Some of the many German reparation ships acquired by New Zealand and Federal came by way of other P. & O. companies, notably the Hain Steamship Co. Ltd. But only during the 1920s and 1930s did the design of the ships for the two companies converge, a trend which was to produce some of the most splendid and characterful cargo liners built anywhere. It is notable that ships which were readily recognizable as descendants of the 1934-built DURHAM served until the companies largely abandoned conventional cargo liner services almost half a century on. New Zealand and Federal were amongst the pioneers of the diesel engine for long-distance routes, and the introduction of the RANGITIKI class of motor passenger liners in 1929 was a particularly bold move. From then on the companies built only motorships whenever possible, the few exceptions being turbine-driven wartime ships, plus some later tankers and a container ship. As well as the stately cargo liners for the main line from Europe to Australasia, diesels also drove the more modest K group, built for the Montreal Australia New Zealand Line Ltd. The M.A.N.Z service was begun in 1936 in conjunction with Port Line and Ellermans to take over a route on which Canadian ships were running unprofitably.

It is scarcely necessary to note that the New Zealand and Federal fleets suffered grievously during the second world war: this was true for most of the world's merchant marines. But the size, power and possibly the impressive appearance of the companies' ships singled them out for trouble.

Some like DORSET and ESSEX were chosen for the hazardous Malta convoys; HORORATA and ROTORUA presented large and tempting targets for U-boats; and even in the remote southern ocean vessels like TURAKINA and RANGITANE were not safe from auxiliary cruisers. The great value of fast modern cargo liners to the war effort meant that the company was allowed to build to its own design during the war. Even these ships suffered and NOTTINGHAM was to disappear on her maiden voyage.

Post-war reconstruction could not have been more energetic, with eight cargo liners being ordered almost immediately and variants on this design appearing in both fleets throughout the 1950s and 1960s. The first years of the post-war period was probably the Golden Age of cargo liner operations; there was relatively little competition for British ships and trade grew in parallel with the increasing affluence of Western Europe, Australasia, and North America. There was even scope for a new operation within the group: Avenue Shipping Co. Ltd. which handled mainly non-refrigerated cargo.

The first clouds to appear over the golden horizon affected the passenger services; the New Zealand company being rather late to realise that loading passengers and cargo on the same ship was no longer a viable proposition. The acquisition of more-or-less dedicated passenger ships came too late as air competition was by then fierce. But the cargo ships were also vulnerable, with their large crews and relatively slow schedules which involved a number of loading and unloading ports. Diversification was tried: as early as 1958 Federal took delivery of tankers, but it seems that the company's heart was never in this business. Amongst the crews there was a feeling that the group was resting on its laurels, certainly as regards their accommodation. In the 1930s, that on the newer ships was amongst the best afloat, but the companies' accommodation was widely bettered in the 1950s.

The first hint of rationalisation - management's typical response to a problem beyond its powers to overcome - was the disappearance of the New Zealand company's funnel colours at the beginning of 1966. Henceforth, all ships would wear Federal colours, and from 1967 they were all registered under Federal ownership. Far worse was to follow. Guided by management consultants, parent P. & O. set out on the ultimate rationalisation in 1971. This saw New Zealand, Federal and Avenue ships, along with those of other companies which had retained their independence under P. & O. ownership for up to half a century, disappear into P. & O. General Cargo Division. Liveries tended to go first, followed by company titles, and - last of all - the New Zealand and English county names; only the Avenue ships succumbing to the tide of STRATH-names. Behind this move, and the subsequent sale or scrapping of most of the cargo liners, was of course containerisation. Even one of the container vessels built for the Australasian services in 1968 - relatively modest, by today's standards - could do the work of ten conventional cargo liners and their large crews.

But just as the last Federal ship had its funnel repainted with P. & O.'s new device, the time-honoured colours were given a reprieve. Probably because of Federal's tradition of operating refrigerated ships, the company's colours - but sadly not its names - were applied to a group of reefers in 1973. But with the disposal of these ships in 1983, almost the last trace of the proud New Zealand/Federal group disappeared. Since the last echo of a New Zealand name for P.&O.'s REMUERA BAY disappeared in 1993 there has been little to remind us of two of the major companies in the important trades between the United Kingdom and Australasia.

Sources and acknowledgements

In writing this brief company history and the individual captions we have drawn on the works listed below.
Duncan Haws, *Merchant Fleets 7: New Zealand Shipping & Federal S.N. Co.*
W.A. Laxon & F.W. Perry, *B.I.: The British India Steam Navigation Co. Ltd.*
John Maber, *North Star to Southern Cross.*
Stephen Rabson & Kevin O'Donoghue, *P. & O.: A Fleet History.*
Ian Stewart, *The Ships that serve New Zealand, Volume 1.*
William Torrance, *Steamers on the River.*
Sydney D. Waters, *Clipper Ship to Motor Liner* and *Ordeal by Sea.*
Facts have been obtained or checked from the usual research sources: *Lloyds Register, Lloyds Confidential Indexes, Lloyds War Loss Books, Lloyds Wreck Books* and *Marine News*.

For helping complete our photographic coverage we would particularly like to thank Cliff Parsons, Keith Byass and Tony Smith of the World Ship Photo Library; Malcolm Cranfield; Fred Hawks; Ian Spashett of Fotoflite and Vic Young. Caption-writing has also benefited from the help of friends, particularly Alan Phipps who recalled his service with Federal, John Hill, Louis Loughran who was consulted over liveries, and John Bartlett who made his superb library available. Use of the resources of the World Ship Society's Central Record and the library of Lloyds Register of Shipping is gratefully acknowledged.

TONGARIRO (1)

John Elder and Co., Govan; 1883, 4163gt, 389 feet

TONGARIRO was the first steamer built for the New Zealand company, receiving a rapturous welcome when she arrived at Port Chalmers in December 1883. At the speed required to maintain a monthly service the ship's compound engines were greedy for coal, reducing her capacity for paying cargo. Nevertheless, TONGARIRO could carry some 27,000 frozen sheep in insulated compartments, and several hundred passengers in accommodation lit by electricity.

TONGARIRO served the New Zealand company until August 1898 when chartered to the Beaver Line for a service from Liverpool to Canada. This company failed after just one year, and TONGARIRO was sold to the British India S.N. Co. Ltd. for Indian Ocean work as ZIBENGHLA, lasting until broken up in Bombay in 1910.

This photograph on the Mersey must date from 1898 or 1899 when TONGARIRO was running for the Beaver Line. Both Beaver and British India used black funnels with two white bands but the bands on the latter's funnels were much closer together than in the photograph.

RUAPEHU (1)

John Elder and Co., Govan; 1883, 4163gt, 389 feet

Sister to TONGARIRO and AORANGI, RUAPEHU was the third steamer built for the company. She gained a certain notoriety in February 1895 when, despite a claimed speed of 14 knots and a fair spread of sails, she was overhauled by the company's sailing ship TURAKINA.

RUAPEHU was sold to the British India S.N. Co. Ltd. in 1899 and renamed ZAYATHLA for the Bay of Bengal trade. However, as with the other ships bought from the New Zealand company, her entry into service was interrupted by the Boer War and the Boxer Rising, during which she became the hospital ship GWALIOR. She retained this name until broken up in Italy during 1911. *[World Ship Photo Library]*

KAIKOURA (1)
John Elder and Co., Govan; 1884, 4474gt, 430 feet

The KAIKOURA class immediately followed the TONGARIRO class but were a size larger, reflecting the huge amount of bunker coal needed for immensely long passages. Rapid developments in marine engineering, and particularly the triple expansion engine, meant that these early steamers were soon outclassed. However, British India again proved a ready buyer, and KAIKOURA became ZAIDA in 1899, working until sold to breakers in Genoa in 1907.

RIMUTAKA (1)
John Elder and Co., Govan; 1884, 4473gt, 430 feet

The considerable length and elegance of the early steamers is apparent in this view of RIMUTAKA. Her career paralleled that of her sister KAIKOURA, and she became British India's ZAMANIA in 1900, going to Japanese breakers in 1911.

WAIKATO (2) *(opposite)*
William Doxford and Sons Ltd., Sunderland; 1892, 4534gt, 400 feet

The clipper bow of the WAIKATO, although romantic, was something of an anachronism by 1892. It was not as if she was an effective sailer: when her propellor shaft broke in the South Atlantic in June 1899 she drifted for four months under sail before a steamer found her and took her in tow. In 1905 WAIKATO was sold to German owners as AUGUSTUS and in 1912 became the Italian TERESA ACCAME. She was broken up in 1923.

THE FIRST FREIGHTERS

OTARAMA (1)
William Doxford and Sons, Sunderland; 1890, 3935gt, 365 feet

OTARAMA was the company's first ship with no passenger accommodation: one of the first results of Dawes' ownership. Her history was rather complex, as she had been built as the straight freighter SEA KING but almost immediately fitted with refrigeration machinery and acquired by the New Zealand company.

The Nelson Line bought her in 1902 and renamed her HIGHLAND GILLIE. She was sold to Hamburg owners in 1912, but was caught in the Black Sea on the outbreak of war in 1914. With little prospect of escape she was sold to the Romanian-based M. Gumuchdjian, who kept her German name CONSTANTIN until 1923 when he transferred her to the British flag as RIVER TYNE. Two years later Gumuchdjian moved her to Belgian registry, and she stayed there as SPA until broken up in Holland in 1933. *[World Ship Photo Library]*

TEKOA (1) *(above)*
Wm. Gray and Co. Ltd., West Hartlepool; 1890, 4050gt, 365 feet

TEKOA was the first ship built for the New Zealand company with triple expansion engines. Despite her modern machinery she was an early sale, going to the Nelson Line as HIGHLAND CORRIE in 1902. She was broken up in Holland during 1909. Such an early scrapping compared with OTARAMA suggests that her machinery was less reliable.

RUAHINE (1)

William Denny and Brothers, Dumbarton; 1891, 6127gt, 430 feet

This splendid shot of RUAHINE undoubtedly shows her on trials in the Clyde, probably whilst running her measured mile on 20th October 1891. Her speed allowed her to improve on her predecessors' passage times, and brought New Zealand within a month of the United Kingdom. Surprisingly, she was sold in 1900, but her new owners - Spain's Compania Transatlantica - ran her across the Atlantic as ANTONIO LOPEZ, and did not break her up until July 1945.

RAKAIA (2)

R. and W. Hawthorn, Leslie and Co. Ltd., Hebburn-on-Tyne; 1895, 5628gt, 420 feet

RAKAIA looks like a pure cargo ship, but actually had accommodation for 250 emigrants in her tween decks. She also had refrigeration machinery, which made her attractive to the infant Blue Star Line, which bought her in 1915 and renamed her BRODMEAD. The usual Vestey Group indecision as to name saw her become ROMANSTAR and later ROMAN STAR. She went to breakers at Savona in 1934.

WAIMATE (2)
R. and W. Hawthorn, Leslie and Co. Ltd., Hebburn-on-Tyne; 1896, 5610gt, 420 feet

WAIMATE and her sisters were a development of the RAKAIA, without the forward well deck. During her career of almost thirty years WAIMATE came through two wars unscathed: the Boer War in which she carried New Zealand troops to South Africa, and the first world war. She was broken up in 1925.

[George Scott collection]

WHAKATANE (1)
R. and W. Hawthorn, Leslie and Co. Ltd., Newcastle; 1900, 5715gt, 420 feet

A sister of WAIMATE, the WHAKATANE was photographed at Dover on 5th July 1909, shortly after a collision with the steamer CIRCE off Dungeness. This photo shows her being pumped out by the LADY CRUNDALL, one of the fine two-funnelled tugs of Dover Harbour Board.

WHAKATANE was repaired and continued with the company until 1924 when she was sold to Italians, for whom she gave five years' service as MONCENISIO before being broken up in Italy.

PAPAROA (1)
William Denny and Brothers, Dumbarton; 1899, 6563gt, 430 feet
After building a series of what were basically large cargo carriers with extensive accommodation for emigrants in the tween decks, the company built two recognisable passenger ships, PAPANUI in 1898 and PAPAROA in 1899. The latter is seen later in her career: she was originally square rigged on her foremast.

PAPAROA was to become one of the company's relatively few peacetime casualties, and even then succumbed to fire rather than stress of weather. Nearing St. Helena on 17th March 1926 whilst on a voyage from the U.K. to Brisbane she was abandoned after catching fire, her passengers and crew being taken off without loss. By a strange coincidence, her sister PAPANUI had caught fire off St. Helena fifteen years earlier.

[World Ship Society collection]

RIMUTAKA (2)

William Denny and Brothers, Dumbarton; 1900, 7952gt, 457 feet

RIMUTAKA is seen in the Mersey, late in her career and after she had been fitted with kingposts in place of cranes ahead of her third hold. She originally carried some 340 passengers in four classes, but the number of passengers and classes was progressively reduced during her long career. She was scrapped at Pembroke Dock in 1930.

TURAKINA (2)

R. and W. Hawthorn, Leslie and Co. Ltd., Hebburn-on-Tyne; 1902, 8349gt, 473 feet

This is TURAKINA in original condition complete with a yard on the foremast, which is reported to have been removed around 1905. She was one of the less fortunate of the four RIMUTAKAs, as on 13th August 1917 she was torpedoed by U-86 in the Western Approaches whilst leaving for New Zealand via the U.S.A. Mercifully there were few casualties among her complement, which included New Zealand troops heading home from the Western Front.

AUSTRALASIAN *(top)* **and RUAPEHU (2)** *(bottom)*
William Denny and Brothers, Dumbarton; 1901, 7885gt, 457 feet

The upper shot is interesting in showing RUAPEHU during 1901 before entering the New Zealand company's service and when she made a few voyages to Canada for Allan Line as AUSTRALASIAN. She is without a yard on her foremast, although a later photograph as RUAPEHU confirms that this was carried. In the lower photograph, RUAPEHU is in New Zealand service, which lasted until she was broken up in Italy during 1931.

FOUR MASTERS

KAIPARA (1)
John Brown and Co. Ltd., Clydebank; 1903, 7392gt, 460 feet

With four masts which gave them a rather Germanic appearance, the twin-screw KAIPARA (top photograph) and her sister KAIKOURA were unusual in the New Zealand fleet.

The centre shot shows the aftermath of an incident in the Rangitoto Channel on 15th January 1910 when KAIPARA grounded soon after leaving Auckland for London. Her cargo of meat, cheese and butter is being unloaded by a wide variety of local craft. KAIPARA was refloated six days later and taken to Christchurch.

KAIPARA's subsequent career was short, and she was a very early first world war loss. On 16th August 1914 she was sunk by the German armed merchant cruiser KAISER WILHELM DER GROSSE off Las Palmas where she was calling for coal on a voyage from Lyttleton via Montevideo to London and Liverpool.

KAIKOURA (2)
John Brown and Co. Ltd., Clydebank; 1903, 6998gt, 460 feet

Although the quality of the negative has deteriorated, it was difficult to resist including this atmospheric shot of KAIKOURA, a Rea tug and a Liverpool dockmaster complete with megaphone. It was probably taken in the early 1920s, before KAIKOURA was sold to Italian owners and renamed first GIANO in 1926 and later FERRANIA. She was demolished at Savona in 1929.

[World Ship Photo Library]

OPAWA (2)

William Denny and Brothers, Dumbarton; 1906, 7230gt, 460 feet

The modest masts of the OPAWA compared with those of her predecessors indicate the use of the Manchester Ship Canal by the New Zealand company. The topmasts were telescopic, and the upper part of her funnel was removable, to allow her to pass below the canal bridges.

Even amongst ships which routinely sailed from one side of the world to the other, OPAWA had an adventurous career. In 1928 she was acquired by Norwegians who converted her to a whale factory ship under the name ANTARCTIC. Later names under Japanese ownership were ANTARCTIC MARU and TONAN MARU. As with so much of Japan's merchant fleet, she fell prey to the Unites States Navy, being sunk by the submarine BOWFIN off what is now Vietnam on 28th November 1943.

OTAKI (2)

William Denny and Brothers, Dumbarton; 1908, 7420gt, 465 feet

Seen here on trials, OTAKI's machinery was novel: the middle one of her three screws was driven by a turbine taking exhaust steam from the triple expansion engines driving the two outboard screws. Despite this profusion of screws and state-of-the-art machinery, she still carried yards for sails on both masts.

OTAKI took part in one the first world war's classic single ship combats. Sunk by the faster and more heavily armed German auxiliary MOEWE in the Atlantic on 10th March 1917, her fight was gallant enough for Captain Bisset-Smith to be awarded a posthumous Victoria Cross: one of very few awarded to merchant seamen. The MOEWE's commander conceded that OTAKI had nearly put his ship out of action, and it took two days to extinguish the fires which her hits had caused.

RUAHINE (2) *(top)* **and AURIGA** *(bottom)*
William Denny and Brothers, Dumbarton; 1909, 10758gt, 481 feet

The twin-screw RUAHINE was the largest New Zealand passenger ship at the time of her completion, and had one of the longest careers of the company's ships, surviving two world wars and several rebuildings. The upper photograph, showing her preparing to leave Liverpool docks, was taken after a 1926 refit in which the deck cranes replaced the derricks to number three hatch and her accommodation was reduced from four classes to simply "tourist". By the late 1930s this outdated accommodation had fallen out of use, but was found useful for second world war troops and post-war emigrants.

The name RUAHINE means "old woman" in Maori, a particularly apt choice in view of her longevity. In 1949, when most ships of her age would be going for scrap, she was sold to Italy and extensively rebuilt to carry emigrants to South America. The lower photograph from October 1955 shows her reincarnated as the AURIGA of Fratelli Grimaldi of Genoa. As this she survived until broken up at Savona in 1957.

ROTORUA (1)
William Denny and Brothers, Dumbarton; 1910, 11130gt, 484 feet

Seen anchored off Tilbury, ROTORUA represented a refinement of the RUAHINE in such details as the derricks to number three hatch, which were carried from new. She also had similar machinery to the Denny-built OTAKI and the same yard arms on fore and main masts. ROTORUA was less fortunate than her running mates, and paid the price of the Admiralty's dilatoriness in implementing a convoy system when torpedoed by UC-17 off Devon on 22nd March 1917.

REMUERA (1)
William Denny and Brothers, Dumbarton; 1911, 11276gt, 485 feet

REMUERA was a sister of ROTORUA, and had the distinction of being the company's first ship to transit the Panama Canal. Her career followed a similar pattern to the lead ship of the group RUAHINE, with her accommodation gradually being downgraded. This photograph, probably at Southampton, shows the REMUERA after her 1920 refit which raised the amidships accommodation by another deck and converted her to oil firing.

On 26th August 1940, REMUERA was nearing home after the long voyage from Wellington with one of the largest cargoes she had lifted. Her convoy had been attacked by U-boats to the north of Scotland, and REMUERA had been appointed the commodore's ship. She was north of Peterhead, crossing the entrance to the Moray Firth, when she was torpedoed by German aircraft. She sank in about three quarters of an hour, but mercifully all her crew escaped and were picked up.   *[George Scott collection]*

FEDERAL'S FIRST NEW BUILDINGS

CORNWALL (1)

R. and W. Hawthorn, Leslie and Co. Ltd., Hebburn-on-Tyne; 1896, 5490gt, 420 feet

CORNWALL was the first ship built for the Federal Steam Navigation Co. Ltd., and with her sister DEVON revived the county names which were one of the company's tenuous links with the famous Money Wigram fleet. She also began Federal's tradition of large and powerful-looking meat carrying ships.

CORNWALL was sold to Italian owners in 1912 and became the ATLANTIDE. On 9th February 1918 she was captured and sunk by U-156 off Madeira whilst on a voyage from Genoa to New Orleans.

[World Ship Society collection]

SURREY (1)

R. and W. Hawthorn, Leslie and Co. Ltd., Hebburn-on-Tyne; 1899, 5455gt, 420 feet

This is SURREY from the second batch of six new Federal ships, which adopted a distinctive style of four tall masts.

SURREY was mined off Calais on 25th February 1915, and beached near Deal. Although declared a constructive total loss, she was sold to the Brodfield Steamship Co. Ltd. - the

embryo Blue Star Line - repaired and renamed BRODFIELD. As this she did not survive long, and was wrecked on the Scillies on 13th November 1916 whilst on a voyage from Le Havre to Barry.

NORFOLK (1)

Sunderland Shipbuilding Co. Ltd., Sunderland; 1900, 5310gt, 421 feet

Near-sister of SURREY, NORFOLK was originally registered in the ownership of Federal's then owners, Birt, Trinder and Bethell. This class dispensed with yards on the foremast, but NORFOLK's captain may have regretted this when she lost her propellor in the Indian Ocean during 1906. Using hatch covers as sails, NORFOLK reached Fremantle where a new screw was fitted.

On 8th November 1914, NORFOLK was less fortunate when she caught fire off the coast of Victoria whilst on an Australian coasting voyage. She was abandoned and drifted ashore to break up on Ninety Mile Beach.

[Eric Johnson/A. Duncan]

SUFFOLK (2)
John Brown and Co. Ltd., Clydebank; 1902, 7317gt, 460 feet

The first SUFFOLK had been wrecked when less than a year old whilst serving as a Boer War transport, and her successor was an even larger ship with twin screws. The second SUFFOLK was registered in the ownership of Birt, Trinder and Bethell; and later Potter, Trinder and Gwyn, but was otherwise part of the fleet of Federal Steam Navigation Co. Ltd, who became the registered owners in 1921. SUFFOLK was broken up on the Clyde by P. & W. MacLellan Ltd. early in 1927.

DORSET (1)
John Brown and Co. Ltd., Clydebank; 1903, 6990gt, 460 feet
The career of DORSET exactly paralleled that of her sister SUFFOLK, with an identical pattern of ownership and going to the same breakers in the same month.

ESSEX (1)
John Brown and Co. Ltd., Clydebank; 1902, 7016gt, 460 feet

ESSEX was a near-sister of the second SUFFOLK, with twin screws. She had accommodation for a large number of emigrants, but 20 cadets replaced these after the first world war. ESSEX was sold to Antwerp owners in 1927 and ran as VAN until broken up on the Clyde in 1933.

SOMERSET (1)
John Brown and Co. Ltd., Clydebank; 1903, 7010gt, 461 feet

This Brisbane view shows SOMERSET before the first world war: she was one of only two Federal-owned ships lost during this conflict. The assailant was U-54, which torpedoed SOMERSET on 26th July 1917 in the Western Approaches whilst she was on a voyage from Buenos Aires to Le Havre with frozen meat. Happily, there were no casualties.   *[V.H. Young and L.A. Sawyer]*

HORORATA (1)
William Denny and Brothers, Dumbarton; 1914, 11243gt, 511 feet

The HORORATA altered the profile of New Zealand ships, which typically had three hatches ahead of the bridge, with a distinct improvement in appearance. A passenger capacity of over 1,000 made her a useful troopship for the Australian Expeditionary Force during the first world war.

During the 1930s HORORATA became yet another of the New Zealand and Federal fleet to carry a complement of cadets. This seems to have attracted her to British India, and she was transferred to their ownership in 1939 and renamed WAROONGA. Alas, she was not to survive her second war, and was torpedoed by U-630 in an eastbound North Atlantic convoy on 5th April 1943 with the loss of 19 of her complement of 132.

SHROPSHIRE *(top)* and **ROTORUA (2)** *(bottom)*
John Brown and Co. Ltd., Clydebank; 1911, 10374gt, 526 feet

Seemingly by agreement, Federal and Bibby used different English county names, and amongst Federal ships only SHROPSHIRE and WILTSHIRE had names ending in -shire to match those of their Scottish Shire Line running mate ARGYLLSHIRE. They were exceptional in build, and appeared massive even in a fleet built to withstand the worst the southern ocean could throw at it. Twin-screw ships with quadruple expansion machinery, they were amongst the largest vessels ever to transit the complete length of the Manchester Ship Canal.

SHROPSHIRE was damaged by a fire in post-war years and was laid up at Falmouth. However, in 1923 she was renamed ROTORUA and extensively converted for service with the New Zealand company which needed a further passenger vessel. Her imposing appearance may have been her undoing, as when serving as commodore ship of inward-bound convoy HX.92 she was torpedoed on 11th December 1940 with the loss of 21 lives whilst approaching Scotland. The commander of U-96 possibly singled her out as an important-looking ship.

WILTSHIRE
John Brown and Co. Ltd., Clydebank; 1912, 10390gt, 567 feet

WILTSHIRE had the shorter career of the two Federal shires. When bound for Auckland on 31st May 1922 she ran onto Great Barrier Island off the North Island of New Zealand in heavy weather. Valiant rescue attempts by other ships over two days succeeded in getting all 103 members of her crew ashore by breeches buoy, but the WILTSHIRE had broken her back and was beyond saving. The subsequent enquiry found her master guilty of a serious error of judgement in proceeding at full speed when uncertain of his position, but because of his conduct following the wreck he was allowed to keep his certificate.

MIDDLESEX (1)
Charles Connell and Co. Ltd., Glasgow; 1914, 7264gt, 470 feet

This is a rare, but unfortunately anonymous, wartime photograph of the first MIDDLESEX in Australia. She was built for Greenshields, Cowie and Co. as KNIGHT BACHELOR, and bought by Federal when only a few months old. The remainder of the fleet of Greenshields, Cowie went to Alfred Holt in 1917.

MIDDLESEX left Manchester in May 1917, bound for Australia, but on 16th May was torpedoed by U-30 north west of Ireland, fortunately without loss of life. *[Roy Fenton collection]*

DEVON (2)
Ateliers et Chantiers de France, Dunkirk; 1915, 9661gt, 473 feet

In 1914 it was highly unusual for a major British cargo liner to be ordered from France. But with shipping booming, British yards had full order books and a French Government subsidy plus early delivery dates helped win the work for the Dunkirk yard. However, with German artillery in range of Dunkirk, DEVON was launched in a hurry and taken to the Thames for completion. Her two intended sisters were eventually completed for French account.

DEVON was originally to have accommodation for emigrants but this seems never to have been used, although she later served as a cadet ship. This led to her being transferred within the P. & O. group in 1934 when she became British India's cadet ship. DEVON not only retained her name, but also remained on Australian services for her new operators. It was on such a voyage that she was caught in the Pacific by the German auxiliary cruiser KOMET on 19th August 1941, sunk by bombs and her crew taken prisoner.

NORTHUMBERLAND (1)
Swan, Hunter and Wigham Richardson Ltd., Newcastle; 1915, 12160 gt, 531 feet

The stumpy masts of the NORTHUMBERLAND - designed to facilitate her passages of the Manchester Ship Canal - combine with her large size to give the impression of a truly massive ship. Her size led to periods of service as a troopship during both wars, and she also served as a cadet ship in succession to DEVON. She held the record as being Federal's largest ship until tankers appeared in the company's colours in the 1960s, and is also reputed to have been the largest ship to visit Manchester. Her long and useful career ended in 1951 at a shipbreaking yard at Inverkeithing.

WESTMORELAND (1)
D. & W. Henderson and Co. Ltd., Glasgow; 1917, 9512gt, 473 feet

This view of the WESTMORELAND at Brisbane emphasises the imposing appearance of contemporary Federal ships. A near-sister of DEVON, but with turbines driving twin screws as in NORTHUMBERLAND, the WESTMORELAND turned out to be built as strongly as she looked, succumbing only to the fourth attack by an enemy.

On 6th February 1918 WESTMORELAND was torpedoed in the Irish Sea but her crew managed to beach her and she was subsequently repaired. Again in the Irish Sea, on 29th January 1941 she struck two mines not far from the Bar Light Vessel, but was rescued and repaired at Liverpool. On 1st June 1942 she was bound from Wellington to Liverpool in convoy when torpedoed by U-566 in the North Atlantic. Her cargo of wool helped keep WESTMORELAND afloat, and it required a second torpedo and shells to finish her off. This allowed time for her crew to get clear in her boats, and there were only three casualties. *[V.H. Young and L.A. Sawyer]*

CORNWALL (2)
William Hamilton and Co. Ltd., Port Glasgow; 1920, 10689gt, 495 feet

Like other contemporary Federal ships, CORNWALL had two sets of turbines driving twin screws, but was distinctly different in appearance. Her machinery arrangement was to prove particularly valuable during CORNWALL's finest hour, in one of the first Malta convoys. On 31st August 1940 the convoy was south of Crete when bombed by Italian aircraft. There were several hits on the CORNWALL, which killed the radio officer, started fires in the ammunition on board, and disabled the steering gear. Within minutes, however, CORNWALL resumed the convoy's speed and course, and steered with her engines until reaching Malta two days later. CORNWALL returned to the relative calm of Australian voyages and - surviving the war - was broken up in 1949 at Briton Ferry.

OTAKI (3)
Barclay Curle and Co. Ltd., Glasgow; 1920, 7964gt, 449 feet

OTAKI began life as the war standard "G" type steamer WAR JUPITER laid down well after the end of the war in 1919. This class was designed as frozen meat carriers, and the New Zealand company needed to make few modifications, although particularly noticeable is the flange to facilitate removing the funnel en route to Manchester.

Pictured here in April 1932, OTAKI had a relatively short career with the New Zealand company, and in her last eight years had four different owners. Late in December 1934 she became Clan Line's CLAN ROBERTSON, passing to Jack Billmeir as STANFLEET in 1938. For a few months in 1939 she was owned by the Zubi Steamship Co. Ltd., a London company with Spanish principals. Her final owners were Blue Star Line Ltd., and as PACIFIC STAR she was torpedoed by U-509 off the Canaries on 28th October 1942. Her complement of 97 got off safely.

PIAKO (2)
Alexander Stephen and Sons Ltd., Linthouse; 1920, 7747gt, 450 feet

PIAKO was originally intended to be WAR ORESTES, a near-sister to OTAKI but with turbines rather than triple expansion machinery, and only a single screw. The turbines probably meant she was retained in the New Zealand fleet when the OTAKI was sold.

PIAKO's otherwise uneventful life of plodding back and forth between U.K. and the Antipodes came to an end on 18th May 1941 when, keeping close to the coast of Africa, she was torpedoed by U-107 with the loss of 10 of her crew.

THE OTARAMA

AJANA *(top)* and **OTARAMA (2)** *(bottom)*
Russell and Co., Port Glasgow; 1912, 7759gt, 454 feet

The Australind Steam Shipping Co. Ltd. was a rather distant relation of Federal and New Zealand Lines, which had a minor stake in the company through managers Trinder, Anderson and Co. One of the few ships transferred between the companies was the AJANA (upper photo), sold to the New Zealand company in 1920 and renamed OTARAMA.

In the lower photograph, OTARAMA is seen in the Mersey with topmasts struck for passage of the Manchester Ship Canal. In 1928 she was sold and became the Italian AMARANTO, and was broken up in 1932.

[Upper: World Ship Society collection]

KENT (2)
Palmers' Shipbuilding and Iron Co. Ltd., Hebburn-on-Tyne; 1918, 9857gt, 461 feet

For a brief period after the first world war, New Zealand and Federal ships had a recognizable style, with long bridge decks. For at least part of their careers, the four turbine-driven Federal ships with this layout had the plating alongside this deck painted white to match the forecastle. They shared with other Federal ships telescopic masts and removable funnel tops for Manchester Ship Canal transits.

The "lucky" KENT was the only one of the Federal quartet to survive the second world war, during which she ran almost exclusively between the U.K. and Australasia, although she made one trip to the Eastern Mediterranean with supplies for Australian troops. In 1950, KENT was felt worthy of a major refit, which took place at Falmouth and involved a new foremast being fitted, together with renewal of shell and deck plating - some of which was actually worn through, allowing water into the holds. Despite this work, in 1955 KENT was broken up at Blyth.

SOMERSET (2)
Earle's Shipbuilding and Engineering Co. Ltd., Hull; 1918, 9773gt, 461 feet

On 11th May 1941 SOMERSET was completing a voyage from the River Plate to Liverpool in convoy SL 72 which was attacked by a Focke-Wulf Fw 200 Condor 300 miles west of Ireland. SOMERSET, leading a column of ships, was singled out for attack, and a bomb stopped her engines and left her sinking. Fortunately, there were no casualties.

[V.H. Young and L.A. Sawyer]

SURREY (2)
Palmers' Shipbuilding and Iron Co. Ltd., Hebburn-on-Tyne; 1919, 9783gt, 460 feet.

SURREY's war story was in complete contrast to that of her sister KENT. During the night of 8th January 1942 she lost both her rudder and her convoy in heavy weather in mid-Atlantic. Following an epic of expert engineering and seamanship, she reached Bermuda on the 30th January with the aid of sails, a jury rudder and several tows. Repairs in the U.S.A. took several months, and she then sailed for Australia with military equipment. She was never to reach her destination. On 10th June 1942 off Central America SURREY was torpedoed by U-68, taking with her 12 of her complement of 75 crew and gunners.

MIDDLESEX (2)
Swan, Hunter and Wigham Richardson Ltd., Newcastle; 1920, 8569gt, 460 feet

The members of the KENT class succumbed to almost every type of hazard during the second world war: marine, submarine, aircraft and, in the case of MIDDLESEX, mine. On 10th January 1941 she was on a coasting voyage from Newport to Swansea when she was mined and sunk off Barry, fortunately without casualties. The MIDDLESEX's master then joined the HUNTINGDON, only to have her torpedoed under him five weeks later.

TEKOA (2)
Earle's Shipbuilding and Engineering Co. Ltd., Hull; 1922, 8526gt, 461 feet

TEKOA was a near-sister of the Kent class, and was the longest-lived of the group. During a career of 36 years with New Zealand Shipping Co. Ltd., she made just 68 voyages - under two a year. In May 1958, whilst laid up at Falmouth, she was bought by the Hector Whaling Co. Ltd. and sent to Wallsend for conversion to a whaling transport. Her new name ENDERBY honoured British whaling pioneers, even though the principals of Hector Whaling were Norwegians. In 1960 the Hector fleet was sold to Japan, and ENDERBY became KYOKUREI MARU, surviving until broken up near Hiroshima in 1969.

TURAKINA (3)
William Hamilton and Co. Ltd., Port Glasgow; 1923, 8565gt, 461 feet

Note how the white forecastle of TURAKINA gives her a rather different appearance from TEKOA. TURAKINA was less fortunate than her sister, and on 20th August 1940 fell in with the German auxiliary cruiser ORION between Sydney and Wellington. TURAKINA's single 4.7 inch gun was no match for the ORION's six 5.9s and, in an action as gallant as that of the OTAKI in the first world war, TURAKINA and 38 of her crew perished. TURAKINA managed to transmit the raider's position, and this may have persuaded the ORION to quit the Tasman Sea so that she had no further successes for several months.

HURUNUI (3)
Sir Raylton Dixon and Co. Ltd., Middlesbrough; 1920, 9266gt, 470 feet

HURUNUI had no sisters in either the Federal fleet, for whom she was ordered, or that of the New Zealand company. The two hatches on the bridge deck are an unusual feature, and these were perpetuated in the design of subsequent company ships. HURUNUI was an early war loss, torpedoed by U-93 on 14th October 1940 in the Western Approaches whilst on a ballast passage from Newcastle to New Zealand. All but two of her crew were rescued. *[V.H. Young and L.A. Sawyer]*

TONGARIRO (3)
William Hamilton and Co. Ltd., Port Glasgow; 1925, 8565gt, 461 feet

Almost the ultimate in long bridge decks was achieved with the TONGARIRO, a development of the KENT class without the well alongside number one hatch. One of the refinements was a hollow rudder which unfortunately sprang a leak in the middle of the North Atlantic during the second world war. It filled with water and, becoming too heavy for the pintles, broke off, leaving the crew with a knotty steering problem in waters infested with U-boats.

The TONGARIRO was one of the company's last turbine steamers, but she outlived most of her immediate motorship successors, and at the age of 35 is reputed to have been able to manage $12^{1}/_{2}$ knots compared with her designed $13^{1}/_{2}$. In 1960 she made her last eastbound voyage, as FAR EAST TRADER, to Hong Kong and the breakers.

CAMBRIDGE (1)
Joh. C. Tecklenborg A.G., Geestemünde; 1916, 10892gt, 525 feet

The group benefited considerably from the acquisition of war reparation tonnage. Amongst those bought from the Shipping Controller in 1921 were five big, twin-screw steamers which had been laid down for Hamburg Amerika Linie during the war, and had little more than delivery mileage on their clocks. All were fitted with refrigeration equipment after purchase by Federal. Oldest of the five was CAMBRIDGE, which had been completed in 1916 as VOGTLAND, and was distinguished by four tall masts.

On 7th November 1940 CAMBRIDGE was on a coasting voyage from Melbourne to Sydney with general cargo from the U.K. when she hit a mine laid a few days before by the German auxiliary cruiser PINGUIN. CAMBRIDGE sank by the stern, but with the exception of the carpenter her crew of 56 got away in the boats and were picked up the next day.

HERTFORD (1)
Bremer Vulkan, Vegesack; 1917, 10117gt, 521 feet

HERTFORD had begun life as Hamburg Amerika's FRIESLAND, and shared the same fate as all Federal's reparation tonnage. Just a month after the CAMBRIDGE had been mined, HERTFORD was severely damaged by another mine laid by the PINGUIN, this time in the entrance to Spencer Gulf. After heroic salvage work HERTFORD was eventually repaired at Sydney, and early in 1942 left for the U.K. Alas, the work was in vain. On 29th March she was proceeding independently towards Halifax when she was torpedoed and sunk by U-571, an attack which resulted in the loss of four lives.

HUNTINGDON (1)
Bremer Vulkan, Vegesack; 1918, 11509gt, 521 feet

The construction of such large ocean-going steamers by Germany shows a remarkable optimism about the outcome of the war: the berths might have been better used for submarines. In fact, work on MUNSTERLAND was suspended before the armistice, and after a considerable time laid up was completed as HUNTINGDON. She ran first as a conventional cargo ship, but was fitted with refrigeration machinery in 1924, being converted from coal to oil firing at the same time.

HUNTINGDON was in a west-bound convoy when torpedoed by U-96 on the night of 23rd February 1941. The crew of 67 got away in the boats and were picked up by a Greek steamer which bravely left the convoy to rescue them.

NORFOLK (2)
Bremer Vulkan, Vegesack; 1918, 10973gt, 521 feet

Completed as SAUERLAND, NORFOLK was similar to HERTFORD, but even though she was built by the same yard a number of detail differences are apparent, most notably the kingpost/ventilators ahead of the bridge.

All the ex-Hamburg Amerika ships in the Federal fleet were destroyed by the country that built them. On 18th June 1941, NORFOLK was sailing independently from South Wales to New Zealand via New York when torpedoed by U-552 about 130 miles west of Barra Head in the Hebrides. With her gun NORFOLK fought back effectively against the now surfaced submarine, but had to be abandoned, allowing U-552 to finish her off with a second torpedo.

CUMBERLAND (2)
Bremer Vulkan, Vegesack; 1919, 11446gt, 520 feet

CUMBERLAND was launched as WENDLAND. Six of Hamburg Amerika's ships were ceded to the U.K., but the RHEINLAND was lost on her delivery voyage.

On 23rd August 1940 CUMBERLAND was outward bound from Liverpool in a 28-ship convoy when attacked by U-57. The position was 20 miles north west of Inistrahull Lighthouse, and it is suggested that the glare of the lighthouse silhouetted the CUMBERLAND. She remained afloat for some

hours and with the exception of four who were killed in the explosion, the crew took to the boats and landed in Ireland.

[Malcolm Cranfield]

TASMANIA
Flensburger Schiffsbau-Gesellschaft, Flensburg; 1913, 7609gt, 485 feet

The ex-German steamers given New Zealand names were much more of a mixed bag than the virtually new Federal ships. TASMANIA had been built for Deutsche-Australische D.G. and retained her route and name when purchased in 1920: a rare case of a company ship not carrying a New Zealand name. Never fitted with refrigerated equipment, she was less useful than the ex-Hamburg Amerika ships in the Federal fleet and was broken up at Rosyth in 1936.

TREVITHICK later PAPANUI (2)
John Brown and Co. Ltd., Clydebank; 1910, 8046gt, 470 feet
TREVITHICK had been built as PREUSSEN for Hamburg Amerika, and was initially acquired from the Shipping Controller by the Hain Steamship Co. Ltd. This company was also by now a member of the P. & O. group, and TREVITHICK was transferred to Federal ownership in 1924, but named as a New Zealand ship, the PAPANUI. Laid up at Falmouth in 1931, she was demolished in Japan during 1933.

PAKIPAKI

Flensburger Schiffsbau-Gesellschaft, Flensburg; 1914, 7233gt, 472 feet

PAKIPAKI followed the same devious route into Federal ownership as PAPANUI. She was originally AMMON of the Deutsche D.G. "Kosmos" of Hamburg, and saw war service as a transport in the Baltic. Hain renamed her TREWINNARD in 1921, and she became Federal-owned in 1924. PAKIPAKI went to Italian breakers in 1933.

PIPIRIKI (1)

Flensburger Schiffsbau-Gesellschaft, Flensburg; 1915, 6804gt, 473 feet

Despite their New Zealand names, the these war reparation ships were placed under Federal ownership. PIPIRIKI had originally been Norddeutscher Lloyd's LIPPE, taking the name TRESITHNEY when joining the P. & O. group. Federal ownership was again short, from 1924 to 1933 when PIPIRIKI - seen here laid up - went to Italian breakers. *[F.W. Hawks]*

PURIRI

Flensburger Schiffsbau-Gesellschaft, Flensburg; 1916, 8047gt, 476 feet

Although built for Norddeutscher Lloyd at the same Flensburg yard as PIPIRIKI, PURIRI hardly appears to be a sister. Previous names were AUGSBURG in German ownership and TREMERE for Hains. Again, service with Federal lasted just ten years, and PURIRI was broken up in Japan in 1934.

[Both F.W. Hawks]

PAREORA (2)

A.G. Weser, Bremen; 1915, 8435gt, 480 feet

PAREORA had begun life as Deutsche D.G. Hansa's FALKENFELS, and was previously Hain's T R E D E N H A M. Federal ownership lasted from 1924 until April 1934 when she arrived at a Japanese breaker's yard. In common with other ships of this group, she is wearing what appear to be P. & O. hull and funnel colours.

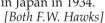

RANGITIKI (2)
John Brown and Co. Ltd., Clydebank; 1929, 16698gt, 531 feet

The three passenger ships which the group built in the late 1920s were amongst the first of their type fitted with diesels, but the motorship fashion for stumpy funnels robbed them of a truly impressive appearance. RANGITIKI's construction was spread over three years, such was the uncertainty of trading conditions, but she and her sister must have been two of the best investments the company made. In the lower view she is seen at Clydebank in October 1947, with a funnel removed whilst the builders replace her engines. This rebuild meant that she served the company until 1962, when she was broken up in Spain.

RANGITIKI's war service as a trooper was outstanding, although in November 1940 she and much of her convoy were saved only through the self-sacrifice of the JERVIS BAY in taking on the German pocket-battleship ADMIRAL SCHEER.

RANGITATA
John Brown and Co. Ltd., Clydebank; 1929, 16737gt, 531 feet

The twin-screw RANGIs were notable not only for being the first of the New Zealand company's ships to employ oil engines, but also because their Brown-Sulzer engines had a largest output per cylinder then achieved. RANGITATA's career almost exactly paralleled that of her sister RANGITIKI: after the war she was re-engined as part of a rebuilding which reduced passenger accommodation from 600 in three classes to around 400 in two. She survived until 1962 when, with her name truncated to RANG, she made her final voyage to breakers in Yugoslavia.

RANGITANE (1)
John Brown and Co. Ltd., Clydebank; 1929, 16733gt, 531 feet

German auxiliary cruisers took the second world war into Australasian waters which, until the Japanese joined the war, were relatively safe from submarines. The third of the company's passenger ships, the RANGITANE, became one of the largest, and certainly the most valuable, victims of this form of warfare when she fell in with the KOMET and ORION (which had recently sunk the TURAKINA) north of New Zealand on 26th November 1940. The auxiliaries' attack was savage, probably in reprisal for the RANGITANE's radio messages, and there were 13 casualties amongst passengers and crew before the firing stopped and the motor liner was evacuated and sunk.

DIESEL CARGO LINERS

OTAIO (1)
Vickers-Armstrongs Ltd., Barrow; 1930, 10048gt, 472 feet

With the RANGIs receiving diesel engines, it was inevitable that this type of propulsion would spread to the cargo liners, although the OTAIO had Doxford engines whilst her sisters had license-built Sulzers like the passenger liners. With their five pairs of kingposts, these twin-screw vessels represented an intermediate stage between the KENT class with their long bridge decks, and the seminal, flush-decked DURHAM class. All the crew were accommodated amidships: perhaps as big an innovation as having diesel engines.

OTAIO succumbed to the carnage which descended on the fleet during the first half of the war. On 28th August 1941, she had just left a west-bound Atlantic convoy to head independently for the Panama Canal and Australia, when she was torpedoed twice by U-558. Fortunately, the convoy was still in sight and its escorts rescued the 58 survivors from the crew of 71.

OPAWA (3)
Alexander Stephen and Sons Ltd., Linthouse; 1931, 10107gt, 471 feet

OPAWA was another, and even more tragic, loss to a U-boat torpedo. On 6th February 1942 she was proceeding independently from Panama to Halifax to join a convoy when she was attacked by U-106, which proceeded to sink her by shell fire once her crew had left. Two of the three boats which got away were never found, and the final toll was 54 lost out of 71.
[World Ship Society collection]

ORARI (3)
Alexander Stephen and Sons Ltd., Linthouse; 1931, 10107gt, 471 feet

Alone amongst the trio, ORARI came through the war, but only just. She was torpedoed south west of Ireland on 13th December 1940 but managed to crawl into the Clyde badly damaged. In June 1942 she was one of the two survivors from a ten-ship Malta convoy, at which the Axis threw everything they had. She reached Malta only to be mined just outside Grand Harbour, but nevertheless delivered her cargo safely. The New Zealand company disposed of her in 1958 but the Italians, who had tried so hard to sink her during the war, ran her as CAPO BIANCO in the South American service until she was scrapped at Savona in 1971. This is a pre-war view of ORARI: she still has kingposts painted the same colour as her masts.

DURHAM (2)
Workman, Clark (1928) Ltd., Belfast; 1934, 10893gt, 494 feet

DURHAM and DORSET must rank as two of the most celebrated of British cargo liners. Not only did they set a style which was to grace the Federal and New Zealand fleets for four decades, but they also had spectacular war careers during which their participation in some of the most heroic Malta convoys ensured their lasting fame.

With their large capacity and speeds of over 16 knots, these twin-screw motorships were natural choices for these convoys. DURHAM survived her heavily-escorted run to Malta in July 1941, but was not so lucky when making her escape. Her troubles began off Cape Bon, Tunisia on 22nd August when she struck one mine and caught another in her paravane. She reached Gibraltar, but on 18th September was attacked by Italian midget submarines which attached explosive charges to her hull. The extensive damage caused by these, added to that from the mine, meant that DURHAM did not return to service until late in 1943.

After the war DURHAM resumed her role as a cadet ship, and at one time no fewer than 21 of the group's ships were commanded by men trained on DURHAM. Her career ended in 1965, but the old lady had only to suffer the indignity of a flag-of-convenience for one voyage to Kaohsiung where she arrived for demolition in March 1966 under the name RION.

DORSET (2)
Workman, Clark (1928) Ltd., Belfast; 1934, 10624gt, 494 feet

In DURHAM and DORSET the long bridge decks which had been a feature of the fleets for many years gave way to a flush-decked layout. Diesel engines and cargo gear comprising two masts plus kingposts to serve other holds were retained from the OTAIO design, and these too were to become trademarks of the group's ships. Sadly, DORSET was the last ship built by the Workman, Clark yard.

DORSET met her end in August 1942 during Operation Pedestal, that supreme effort to fight supplies through from Gibraltar to Malta. After numerous and heavy air attacks, DORSET lost contact with the convoy after dark on 12th August, and survived mine explosions and an E-boat attack. She rejoined the convoy next day, but a determined air attack during the morning caused damage and fires, which threatened to ignite the aviation spirit on board and she had to be abandoned. Although only five of the 14 merchant ships which set out from Gibraltar reached Malta, the cargoes that did get through helped the island play a decisive role in the eventual victory in North Africa.

ESSEX (2) *(top)*, PARINGA *(centre)* and NORFOLK (4) *(bottom)*

John Brown and Co. Ltd., Clydebank; 1936, 11063gt, 532 feet

The ESSEX class was a further refinement of the DURHAM, twin-screw vessels with Doxford diesels which could push them along at $19^1/_2$ knots. ESSEX had some identity problems: she was intended to have been named PAPANUI, and her official owners were P. & O., who bareboat chartered her to Federal.

It was her speed and capacity which selected the ESSEX for a Malta convoy in January 1941. With a heavy escort, the convoy was fought through to the island, but once there ESSEX was repeatedly bombed, unfortunately with the loss of 16 lives. She eventually left Malta in August 1943 and was towed to Falmouth for repairs, which were not completed until November 1944.

ESSEX's nominal owners took her over in 1946, and she sailed on their Australian service as PARINGA. Returned to Federal colours in May 1955, there was by now another ESSEX in service, so she took the name NORFOLK. As such she was sold to Japanese breakers in 1962.

SUSSEX (3) *(top)*, **PALANA** *(centre)* **and CAMBRIDGE (2)** *(bottom)*
John Brown and Co. Ltd., Clydebank; 1937, 11063gt, 532 feet

SUSSEX was the first of the group's ships to suffer enemy action when she hit a magnetic mine off Southend on 24th November 1939. Repaired, she was damaged by bombs from a Focke-Wulf Fw 200 Condor west of Ireland on 30th September 1940, but the attacker was fought off and she brought her valuable cargo into the Clyde.

Her ownership and peacetime life paralleled that of ESSEX. Owned officially by P. & O., she was intended to have been PAREORA and to wear New Zealand colours. In 1946 she was painted in P. & O.'s colours to become PALANA, and ran on their Australian services until 1954. She was then repainted in Federal colours and served as CAMBRIDGE until broken up in Japan in 1962.

SUFFOLK (3)
John Brown and Co. Ltd., Clydebank; 1939, 11145gt, 551 feet

SUFFOLK was ready for sea on 2nd September 1939, the day before the second world war started, and her immaculate paint work was immediately covered in a coat of wartime grey. As something of a war baby, SUFFOLK came through completely unscathed by enemy action, having completed a creditable 16 round voyages to the antipodes, during which she delivered men and supplies to a number of hot spots, including Malta.

Her peacetime service was equally solid, her final voyage being to the breakers in Kaohsiung in 1968.

HORORATA (2)
John Brown and Co. Ltd., Clydebank; 1942, 13945gt, 532 feet

HORORATA had no true sisters, and she is best regarded as an enlarged ESSEX, with modifications. The most fundamental of these was the substitution of turbines for diesels, but outwardly she was distinguished by the lack of a mainmast, and the absence of rake to funnel and foremast. Her upright appearance has been explained as a way of confusing the enemy about the direction she was steaming, but it is questionable whether this could ever be in doubt with a 16-knot steamer. Certainly, U-103 had little problem in torpedoing her north-west of the Azores on 13th December 1942. With two holds flooded, HORORATA reached Flores and later Horta where, with primitive facilities and much ingenuity, she was patched, largely with timber which was growing locally. HORORATA eventually sailed for Liverpool on 17th March 1943.

The utilitarian appearance of HORORATA was matched by such details as no wooden capping to the rails and a lack of wooden decking in the accommodation; features which meant her crew referred to her as "Horor-rata". Her career ended in 1967 when she arrived at Kaohsiung for demolition, having made her last voyage under the Greek flag as NOR.

THE RIMUTAKA

RIMUTAKA (3) *(top and centre)* **and NASSAU** *(bottom)*
Sir W.G. Armstrong, Whitworth and Co. Ltd., Newcastle; 1923, 16385gt, 552 feet

RIMUTAKA was a stop gap, chartered from P. & O. in 1938 as a replacement for the second RUAHINE. She began life as MONGOLIA on the London to Australia service, but as the depression began to bite her accommodation was gradually downgraded, ultimately becoming tourist class only. She was laid up, awaiting sale, when the opportunity arose to use her on New Zealand services. She continued to run to New Zealand for most of the war, also making a trooping voyage from time to time.

In 1950 with newer passenger ships coming into service, RIMUTAKA was sold, but the ageing lady still had plenty of life left. As the Panama-flag EUROPA she ran between Antwerp and New York, but in 1951 she was transferred to Liberian registry and as NASSAU cruised out of New York, as in the bottom photo taken in June 1953. In 1961 Mexican interests bought her, and she was refitted by Fairfields at Glasgow. As ACAPULCO she was not a great success, however, and her next buyers were Japanese breakers who took delivery late in 1964.   *[Middle: George Scott collection]*

ARDENVOHR *(top)*, **KAIMATA** *(centre)* **and ANTRIM** *(bottom)*
William Denny and Bros. Ltd., Dumbarton; 1931, 5237gt, 416 feet

From 1937 the New Zealand company acquired or built five motorships to take their share of the Montreal Australia New Zealand Line Ltd. (MANZ) service which had previously been operated by Canadian ships. Each of the ships was given a name starting with the letter K.

ARDENVOHR came first. She had been built as a speculation by Denny, who entrusted management to Trinder, Anderson and Co. New Zealand Shipping Co. Ltd. bought her in 1937 and after a short period renamed her KAIMATA, repainting her in their own colours but leaving her management unchanged.

When the Avenue Shipping Co. Ltd. was reactivated in 1954 (see page 86), the K group were transferred and continued under Trinder, Anderson management. KAIMATA became ANTRIM, but remained with Avenue for just three years, being sold to Hong Kong owners in 1957 to become HONGKONG FIR. In 1962 she was bought by Indonesia and successively renamed ADRI X, AFFAN ELBAHAR in 1963, and SANG PRATIWI in 1965. She was broken up in 1969.

KAIKOURA (3) *(top)* **and TYRONE** *(bottom)*
Alexander Stephen and Sons Ltd., Linthouse; 1937, 5852gt, 460 feet

KAIKOURA was the first new ship delivered for the MANZ service; a neat, modern-looking motor vessel. Port Line also built motorships for its share of the service, although the third partner, Ellerman, used its existing tonnage.

The New Zealand Ks were all repainted as Avenue ships in 1954 or 1955, and KAIKOURA became TYRONE. In the bottom photograph, note the Trinder, Anderson flag at the foremast. Flying the houseflag here was an unusual tradition carried on by Avenue ships but not by those of Trinder, Anderson's own Australind Steam Shipping Co. Ltd.

TYRONE was to see out her life in Avenue colours, arriving at Hong Kong and the breakers in 1963.

[Top: V.H. Young and L.A. Sawyer]

KAIPAKI *(top)* **and WESTMEATH** *(bottom)*
Alexander Stephen and Sons Ltd., Linthouse; 1939, 5862gt, 459 feet

KAIPAKI is seen here in Brisbane. The Australasia to Canada service of these ships meant they were rather unpopular with British crews, who could be away from home for up to two years at a time.

KAIPAKI was a virtual sister of KAIKOURA, and had a similar career, being transferred to Avenue Shipping Co. Ltd. in 1955 to become WESTMEATH. She too finished her days with Avenue, and arrived at Antwerp for breaking up just after Christmas 1962. *[Top: V.H. Young and L.A. Sawyer]*

KAIPARA (2) *(top)* and ROSCOMMON *(bottom)*
William Doxford and Sons Ltd., Sunderland; 1938, 5882gt, 455 feet

Also seen at Brisbane, KAIPARA was a Doxford interpretation of the KAIPARA design. Note the elimination of the kingposts/ventilators behind the bridge. On going to Avenue in 1955 she became ROSCOMMON, and when leaving this fleet in 1962 she sailed under the Lebanese flag as CRIS until broken up at Kaohsiung in 1967.

[Top: V.H. Young and L.A. Sawyer]

KAITUNA (top) and ARMAGH (bottom)
Eriksberg M.V. Aktieb., Gothenburg; 1938, 4907gt, 432 feet

The KAITUNA, a further variation on the K design, arrived from Sweden in December 1938. Note the Scandinavian builders' trade mark of a pleasing wooden bridge front. KAITUNA is seen in floating dry dock at Wellington during the 1950s.

Like her sisters, KAITUNA's career held no surprises: she went to Avenue in 1954 as ARMAGH, was sold in 1961 and finished her days as the Hong Kong-owned SHUN WAH. She was damaged by a collision with a tug in November 1966, and broken up at Nagasaki early in 1967.   *[Top: V.H. Young and L.A. Sawyer]*

GLOUCESTER
Alexander Stephen and Sons Ltd., Linthouse; 1941, 8532gt, 473 feet

With its heavy losses, and the value of fast cargo liners to the war effort, it was not surprising that the company was allowed to build their own ships during wartime. What is surprising is that time and effort was spent on producing an entirely new, albeit somewhat simplified, design. GLOUCESTER was a single-screw motorship capable of 14 knots. Her cargo gear, too, was less sophisticated than her immediate John Brown-built predecessors. A short, but full height, forecastle was another departure from previous designs.

GLOUCESTER's wartime career was to include voyages to Australasia as well as taking supplies to combat areas, including Algeria in late 1942 and the Pacific. Her lack of sophistication meant that her peacetime career, although creditable, was not as long as other company ships, and she was sold as the WESTMORLAND class began to be delivered. In 1966 she went to Panama owners as CONSULATE for a voyage to Hong Kong, from where she was towed to Kaohsiung for scrap.

NOTTINGHAM (1)
Alexander Stephen and Sons Ltd., Linthouse; 1941, 8532gt, 473 feet

On initial examination, the scruffy appearance of NOTTINGHAM suggested this shot was taken after one or more voyages. Tragically, however, NOTTINGHAM could only have been photographed in the Clyde once, late in October 1941 and probably on her trials. She set out independently for New York on 1st November and seven days later radioed that she had been torpedoed south east of Greenland. There were no survivors amongst the 62 on board, making the NOTTINGHAM's loss the single worst disaster in the group's history. The submarine responsible was U-74.

PAPANUI (3)
Alexander Stephen and Sons Ltd., Linthouse; 1943, 10002gt, 494 feet

Stephens continued to build ships for the company throughout and beyond the second world war. PAPANUI and her sisters were lengthened versions of GLOUCESTER, with single screws driven by three sets of turbines which gave them a speed of about 15 knots.

In January 1952 PAPANUI went to the aid of THOULA CHANDRIS, which was drifting in the Tasman Sea with her boiler room flooded, and towed her into Nelson. This elderly, former Union Steamship Co., steamer had just been sold to the Chandris group.

These two photographs of PAPANUI provide an interesting contrast. In the upper, her sinews appear stiffened for war, with gun mountings, carley floats, no fore or main topmasts, and a short funnel. In the lower shot, leaving Swansea, she is in the full glory of the New Zealand company's simple but dignified livery. As with many of the company's ships, at the end of her career PAPANUI was sold to make one last eastbound voyage. As the Greek-owned FLISVOS she arrived at Kaohsiung in October 1965.

PAPAROA (2)
Alexander Stephen and Sons Ltd., Linthouse; 1944, 10005gt, 491 feet

In the top photo, although she can be little more than a year old, PAPAROA looks somewhat war weary with her hull streaked with dirt and rust. Note also the limited forward visibility from her wheelhouse.

In June 1962 PAPAROA became famous for the usual 15 minutes when she crawled into Port Elizabeth with three of her four propellor blades damaged. It was assumed she had hit a submarine, and this being the time of the cold war, that it was a Russian one. PAPAROA was transferred to Federal ownership and colours in 1967, and in 1970 put under the Greek flag for her last voyage to breakers in Taiwan as MARGARET.

PIPIRIKI (2)
Alexander Stephen and Sons Ltd., Linthouse; 1944, 10057gt, 494 feet

With their tall, straight funnels and upright masts this class always appeared a little anachronistic. Interestingly, in the top photograph in war rig PIPIRIKI looks sleeker and more purposeful, largely due to the short, cowl-topped funnel and the absence of top hamper. The centre picture shows her arriving at Brisbane from the U.S.A. in March 1959. After a few years in Federal ownership and livery as in the bottom photo, PIPIRIKI was sold east and broken up at Kaohsiung in 1971.

DORSET (3)
Alexander Stephen and Sons Ltd., Linthouse; 1949, 10108gt, 495 feet

In 1949 Stephens produced a steam turbine ship with a hull similar to those of the GLOUCESTER class, but to peacetime standards, and with extra cargo gear. DORSET traded mainly to Australia, although she is seen here off Wellington in May 1970. She was sold to Hamburg breakers in 1972 but they resold her, and she was eventually demolished on the Golden Horn, Istanbul's romantic-sounding waterway which is little more than a ships' graveyard.

DEVON (3)
Alexander Stephen and Sons Ltd., Linthouse; 1946, 9940gt, 495feet

The construction of DORSET and DEVON benefited from Stephen's wartime experience, and the ships incorporated a greater degree of prefabrication than their New Zealand sisters. DEVON's service was quite varied, and during the 1960s she took occasional sailings for the MANZ service and for Crusader Shipping Co. Ltd. In 1967, for reasons best known to accountants, she was transferred to the ownership of Overseas Container Lines Ltd. for two years. DEVON was broken up at Hong Kong in 1971.

SOMERSET (3) *(top)* **and ADEN** *(bottom)*
Alexander Stephen and Sons Ltd., Linthouse; 1946, 9943gt, 495 feet

Although never formally transferred to P. & O. ownership, SOMERSET spent most of her career in their colours as ADEN. She took the name ADEN in 1954, being exchanged for PARINGA which was transferred to Federal and became NORFOLK. ADEN was demolished at Kaohsiung in 1967.

[Top: V.H. Young and L.A. Sawyer; bottom: World Ship Society collection]

SAMESK *(top)* **and LEICESTER** *(bottom)*
Bethlehem Fairfield Shipyard Inc., Baltimore; 1944, 7266gt, 424 feet

The Liberty LEICESTER was in Federal ownership for only three years from 1947 to 1950, yet in that time she achieved considerable notoriety. She was on a ballast voyage from Tilbury to New York when, on the night of 14th September 1948, she ran into a hurricane. Because Liberties were regarded as stiff ships, it was the practice to place solid ballast in their tween decks. In the hurricane, LEICESTER's shifting boards gave way and the ballast moved, causing a list which at times was reportedly as bad as 70 degrees. Her crew abandoned her, but six lives were lost. The LEICESTER was made of stout stuff, however, and she was sighted still afloat four days later and was eventually towed into Bermuda. The group had other unhappy experiences with its managed Liberties: the SAMSIP was mined in the Scheldt in December 1944, and the SAMKEY disappeared in January 1948 on a similar voyage to LEICESTER.

LEICESTER had been built as SAMESK for charter to the Ministry of War Transport, who entrusted management to the New Zealand Shipping Co. Ltd. She was bought by Federal and renamed in 1948. After her sale in 1950 she became the British-flag INAGUA, passing in 1958 to Ante Topic who renamed her first SERAFIN TOPIC and then JELA TOPIC, both under the Liberian flag. Her final name, adopted in 1965, was VIKING LIBERTY but in January 1966 she grounded off Trinidad, and was fit only for breaking up, arriving at Santander in August 1966. *[Top: World Ship Society collection; bottom: Fotoflite incorporating Skyfotos]*

STAFFORD

J.A. Jones Construction Co. Inc., Brunswick, Georgia; 1944, 7296gt, 424 feet

The two Liberties owned by Federal had the rare distinction of carrying names used by no other members of the fleet, although the Bibby Line had similar names. Built as SAMINGOY, STAFFORD's career paralleled that of LEICESTER, even being sold in 1950 to the same Bahamas-based owners who renamed her BIMINI under the British flag. As the Panama flag HERNAN CORTES she stranded off Yucatan, Mexico in October 1966. By coincidence this was within months of her sister's stranding off Trinidad. Breakers in Puerto Rico dismantled HERNAN CORTES in August 1967. *[F.W. Hawks]*

EMPIRE WINDRUSH

Blohm und Voss, Hamburg; 1931, 14414gt, 501 feet

In contrast to their large fleet of reparation ships after the previous conflict, the New Zealand and Federal companies gained only one ship from Germany after the second world war, and she was managed for the Ministry of Transport. The motorship EMPIRE WINDRUSH had been built as MONTE ROSA for the River Plate service of the Hamburg-Südamerikanische D.G. Her war service was very mixed, and she was used as an accommodation ship, a repair ship, a troop transport and finally a hospital ship, as which she was mined in February 1945.

She was taken over by the British at the end of the war, and after repairs emerged as a troopship which was allocated to the New Zealand company to manage. EMPIRE WINDRUSH made trooping voyages to the Middle and Far East, and attended the Spithead Coronation Review. Her end was to be violent: a fire broke out in her engine room whilst homeward bound off Algeria on 28th March 1954. Four of her crew were killed, and EMPIRE WINDRUSH sank the next day.

EMPIRE ABERCORN *(centre)* and
RAKAIA (3) *(top and bottom)*
*Harland and Wolff Ltd., Belfast; 1945,
8563gt, 474 feet*

EMPIRE ABERCORN was one of a number of long bridge deck, single-screw, refrigerator ships built at Belfast. Others served in the Union Castle and Blue Star fleets. She was managed for the Ministry of War Transport by the New Zealand company, who bought and renamed her RAKAIA in 1946. Originally she had basic accommodation for 45 passengers, but after 1950 this was refitted for the use of 40 cadets.

An incident in October 1957 showed that the improvisatory spirit that brought the HORORATA home was still alive. A day and a half out from New York a broken piston rod severely damaged RAKAIA's diesel engine, leaving her capable of only 3½ knots. To steady the ship the cadets were set to make sails from hatch covers, and with the help of these she reached Liverpool safely. RAKAIA was broken up at Hong Kong during 1971.

The top photograph shows her arriving at Brisbane from the U.S.A. in September 1959; the bottom shot laid up in the Fal in Federal colours exactly ten years later.

*[Centre: V.H. Young and
L.A. Sawyer]*

NORFOLK (3) *(top)* **and HAURAKI** *(bottom)*
John Brown and Co. Ltd., Clydebank; 1947, 11272gt, 561 feet

With the NORFOLK the fleet began its post-war reconstruction. The six-hold design was based on the pre-war ESSEX class, with similar Doxford diesels driving twin screws, but with the addition of a forecastle. They were splendid-looking ships in the group's best tradition, but the standard of her finish meant NORFOLK did not endear herself to her seamen. Their mess had no hot water, which had to be brought in a bucket from the washrooms; and was prone to flooding when a big sea filled the starboard alleyway. Another annoying feature was a loose rivet trapped in the foremast yardarm, which rattled noisily from end to end in rough weather.

The NORFOLK was delivered in Federal colours, but in 1953 was repainted and renamed HAURAKI as a unit of the New Zealand fleet. Presumably this was to suit conference arrangements as she remained in Federal ownership, and indeed reverted to their colours in 1966. She arrived at Kaohsiung for demolition late in 1973, now registered in the ownership of P. & O.

HAPARANGI
John Brown and Co. Ltd., Clydebank; 1947, 11281gt, 561 feet

HAPARANGI was completed nine months after the lead ship, but the group was dubbed the HAPARANGI class after NORFOLK was renamed HAURAKI.

Seen in the upper photograph in July 1965, HAPARANGI achieved a creditable 26 years service to Australasia. Gradual rationalisation by P. & O. saw her transferred first to Federal ownership and funnel colours, as in the lower photograph, and finally to P. & O. themselves. She was demolished in Taiwan during 1974.

HURUNUI (4)
Vickers-Armstrongs Ltd., Newcastle; 1948, 11276gt, 561 feet

HURUNUI is remembered by those who served on her as being finished to a higher standard than the lead ship of her class, NORFOLK. For example, the joggled deck plates gave a flush surface, preventing the crew tripping over raised edges. Seen here in the Brisbane River during August 1954, HURUNUI lasted 25 years and was broken up in South Korea during 1973.

HUNTINGDON (2)
Alexander Stephen and Sons Ltd., Linthouse; 1948, 11281gt, 561 feet

HUNTINGDON served Federal and, briefly, P. & O. until 1975 when she arrived at Taiwan to be demolished.

HINAKURA
John Brown and Co. Ltd., Clydebank; 1949, 11272gt, 561 feet

HINAKURA's progress through life was marked by little more excitement than the same changes of funnel colours and official ownership which her sisters experienced. She began life in New Zealand colours, as in the top photograph taken in February 1953. She was given a Federal funnel in 1966 as in the centre photo dated September 1967, transferred to their ownership a year later, painted in P. & O. colours and assumed their ownership in 1973 as shown in bottom photo taken in November 1973. Her career ended at a Kaohsiung scrap yard in 1974.

CUMBERLAND (3)

Alexander Stephen and Sons Ltd., Linthouse; 1948; 11281gt, 561 feet

Despite the uniformity of Federal ships, there were occasional variations, and one bosun always painted the funnel of his particular ship a lighter shade. His presence on the CUMBERLAND was apparent whilst she was strike-bound with three other of the class in Wellington during 1952. Traditionally, cleaning and painting the funnel was the regular job for the crew on the first full day after arriving in New Zealand.

CUMBERLAND is seen here at Wellington in the summer sunshine of the Southern Hemisphere in January 1972. The sun finally set for her on Christmas Day 1976 when she arrived at Kaohsiung for demolition.

HERTFORD (2)

Vickers-Armstrongs Ltd., Newcastle; 1948, 11276gt, 561 feet

Remarkably, HERTFORD was the sole member of this eight-ship class to trade for other owners, and then only briefly. In 1976, as her sisters headed east for the breakers, she hoisted the Cypriot flag as THIA DESPINA. On 9th July 1977 she stranded at Suez and suffered damage which led to her being taken to Piraeus and laid up. Although she was sold and renamed GEORGIOS FRANGAKIS, she was not to trade again but was taken to Aliaga and broken up. HERTFORD is shown here passing Portishead in April 1969.   *[Malcolm Cranfield]*

SUSSEX (4)

John Brown and Co. Ltd., Clydebank; 1949, 11272gt, 561 feet

Seen here at Swansea in June 1958, SUSSEX is in the Federal colours which suited her best - with masts distinguished from kingposts and with a white line on her hull. After a few years in P. & O.'s less successful colour scheme, SUSSEX was sold to a Hong Kong scrap yard towards the end of 1976.

RANGITOTO
Vickers-Armstrongs Ltd., Newcastle; 1949, 21809gt, 609 feet

Perhaps wisely, the New Zealand company made replacement of its cargo ships its major priority after the second world war. Passenger ships came along after the HAPARANGIs, and to a large extent were extended versions of the cargo liners. They could carry almost as much cargo as well as having accommodation for over 400 passengers in one class.

RANGITOTO was sold in August 1969 to the C.Y. Tung group, and was modified to become the ORIENTAL CARNAVAL. Her round-the-world service was short-lived, however, and in 1975 she was laid up in Hong Kong and demolished there in 1976. *[Fotoflite incorporating Skyfotos]*

RANGITANE (2)
John Brown and Co. Ltd., Clydebank; 1949, 21867gt, 609 feet

In service RANGITOTO and sister RANGITANE embarked passengers in London and, sailing via the Panama Canal, took about 30 days to reach Wellington or Auckland, where RANGITANE is seen here. Returning to the U.K., passengers and mail were unloaded at Southampton.

First of the New Zealand passenger ships to be withdrawn, RANGITANE was sold for scrapping in 1968 and voyaged east as JAN. However, she was saved at the eleventh hour, and followed her near sisters into the fleet of C.Y. Tung as ORIENTAL ESMERALDA. She was eventually broken up at Kaohsiung in 1976.

[Malcolm Cranfield]

RUAHINE (3)
John Brown and Co. Ltd., Clydebank; 1951, 17851gt, 585 feet

RUAHINE was a slightly smaller version of RANGITOTO with passenger accommodation reduced by one third. The combining of cargo and passengers in these ships meant that the accommodation was unused for lengthy periods while the ship was loading and discharging on the coasts of New Zealand and the U.K. It is interesting to recall that one year after RUAHINE's delivery, competitors Shaw, Savill ordered a pure passenger ship for the same route, the SOUTHERN CROSS. The New Zealand ships were particularly vulnerable to industrial action by dockers or wharfies, as to keep to their passenger schedules they had to sail whether or not their cargo was loaded. This was blamed for hastening the end of the passenger service, but in reality it had been unprofitable for several years.

The passenger ships spent their last years in Federal colours, as seen in the lower photograph. RUAHINE was only 17 years old when sold in 1968, and with minor modifications saw out her life as C.Y. Tung's ORIENTAL RIO, being demolished in Kaohsiung during 1973.

REMUERA (2) *(top),*
PARTHIA *(centre)* and
ARAMAC *(bottom)*
Harland and Wolff Ltd., Belfast;
1948, 13619gt, 534 feet

Sale of the aged RANGITIKI and RANGITATA in 1962 left gaps in the company's passenger schedule which were partly filled by the acquisition of Cunard's intermediate liner PARTHIA, which was expensively refitted at Linthouse and became REMUERA. But the airliners which had driven the PARTHIA off the North Atlantic soon caught up with

her on the New Zealand service and in 1965, after only six round voyages, she was transferred within the P. & O. group to the Eastern and Australian Steamship Co. Ltd. As the ARAMAC she found some employment running between Australia and South East Asia, until arriving at Kaohsiung to be broken up in 1969.

[Middle: Fotoflite incorporating Skyfotos]

NOTTINGHAM (2)
John Brown and Co. Ltd., Clydebank; 1950, 6689gt, 480 feet

In the early 1950s Federal built a group of four ships with limited refrigerated space designed principally for service to smaller Australian ports where draft was restricted. NOTTINGHAM was something of a prototype, and was given a single six-cylinder Doxford diesel. By a narrow margin she was Federal's smallest ship. One notable departure from her Australasian trading was the year which NOTTINGHAM spent on charter to the People's Republic of China beginning in 1959. She was broken up at Taiwan in 1971.

CORNWALL (3)
Alexander Stephen and Sons Ltd., Linthouse; 1952, 7583gt, 489 feet

After a short lull, Alexander Stephen turned out three ships a few feet longer than NOTTINGHAM. External differences included three extra pairs of kingposts, but internal differences were more fundamental, with a pair of eight-cylinder Sulzer diesels driving one shaft through electro-magnetic couplings. The company had met this type of machinery when operating the EMPIRE WINDRUSH. CORNWALL was transferred to British India S.N. Co. Ltd. in August 1967, and as JUNA continued to run from Australia and New Zealand, but now mainly to India and the Persian Gulf. She was broken up at Kaohsiung in 1971.

SURREY (3) *(top)* **and JUWARA** *(bottom)*
Alexander Stephen and Sons Ltd., Linthouse; 1952, 8227gt, 499 feet

Built to the same basic design as CORNWALL, SURREY was longer in both hull and engines, the latter comprising two nine-cylinder Sulzers. This installation seems to have given more trouble than CORNWALL's, and SURREY had to make at least two voyages home from Australia on one engine. This at least demonstrated the flexibility of the two-engine layout. A further advantage of this machinery was that when manoeuvring one engine could be kept running astern with the other running ahead and the gearing quickly switched as appropriate.

Sale to the British India S.N. Co. Ltd. in September 1969 was followed by just three years' service as JUWARA, and she was broken up at Kaohsiung in 1972.

MIDDLESEX (3) *(top)* **and JELUNGA** *(bottom)*
Alexander Stephen and Sons Ltd., Linthouse; 1952, 8284gt, 499 feet

MIDDLESEX had even more cylinders than SURREY: ten to each engine. One of these Sulzers was actually built in the heart of Europe at Winterthur, and brought to Scotland for installation. The other, more sensibly, was made under licence by her hull builders. Seen in the upper photo at Halifax, Nova Scotia, MIDDLESEX had the longest career of the group. British India bought her and named her JELUNGA in November 1968, and she survived to suffer P. & O.'s rampant urge for corporate identity, which put her in their ownership and colours in 1973, as seen in the lower photo at Wellington in 1974. She was renamed STRATHLEVEN in 1975 and given a corn-coloured hull. By the time of her sale for demolition in 1977, Gadani Beach breakers were making the running, and these gentlemen dismantled her early in 1978.

NORTHUMBERLAND (2) *(top and centre)* **and GOLDEN CITY** *(bottom)*
John Brown and Co. (Clydebank) Ltd., Clydebank; 1955, 10335gt, 499 feet.

Shown first in 1959, NORTHUMBERLAND was a logical development of the MIDDLESEX, with an increase in crew accommodation achieved by extending the superstructure aft around the fourth hatch. She was originally intended to be TURAKINA for the New Zealand company.

The centre photograph shows NORTHUMBERLAND in the colours of Crusader Shipping Co. Ltd. in February 1971. This company began operating in 1958, to provide a refrigerated and general cargo service between New Zealand and South East Asia and the West Coast of the U.S.A. The company had its own ships, but others were provided by the joint owners, Blue Star, New Zealand, Port and Shaw, Savill Lines.

NORTHUMBERLAND was sold in 1972, first becoming the KAVO ASTRAPI of the Greek Gourdomichalis group. In 1973 she was sold to Guan Guan (Shipping) Pte. as GOLDEN CITY, as seen in the bottom photograph at Singapore during March 1975. GOLDEN CITY was broken up in Hong Kong during 1978.

OTAKI (4)

John Brown and Co. (Clydebank) Ltd., Clydebank; 1953, 10934gt, 526 feet

OTAKI and ESSEX took their six-hold layout from the HAPARANGI class but their machinery derived from the success of the CORNWALLs, with two twelve-cylinder Sulzers geared to one shaft. The superstructure grew; the bridge being one deck higher and accommodation being trunked around the fourth hatch so that most members of the crew had their own cabin. A nice touch was the display in her dining saloon of the Victoria Cross won by the second OTAKI's master. OTAKI is seen leaving Brisbane in October 1957.

In 1975 OTAKI was sold to Roussos Brothers of Piraeus, who placed her under the Cyprus flag as MAHMOUT, but whilst refitting for this owner at Perama she caught fire and was laid up as a constructive total loss. Although she was sold and renamed NATALIA in 1979, her only move was in tow to Izmir, Turkey for demolition in 1984.

ESSEX (3)

John Brown and Co. (Clydebank) Ltd., Clydebank; 1954, 10936gt, 526 feet

ESSEX is seen arriving at Brisbane in July 1961. Sold simultaneously with her sister OTAKI in December 1975, ESSEX became the GOLDEN GULF of Guan Guan Shipping (Pte.) Ltd., of Singapore. She was demolished at Gadani Beach towards the end of 1977.

WHAKATANE (2) *(top)* **and WAITAKI** *(bottom)*
Alexander Stephen and Sons Ltd., Linthouse; 1954, 8726gt, 472 feet

In the 1950s three partially-refrigerated ships were built mainly for the trade from Australasia to the east coast ports of the U.S.A., an important destination for New Zealand meat. They were of a size with the smaller Federal ships, but were distinguished by their long forecastles. They could carry just six passengers.

Two of the ships were sold to the Union Steam Ship Co. Ltd. of New Zealand Ltd. in 1964 and 1965: in effect an internal transfer as this company had been owned by P. & O. since 1917. WHAKATANE became WAITAKI for the New Zealand to Calcutta trade run jointly by the Union company and British India. Sold in 1970, she carried the names SUCCESSFUL ENTERPRISE, WAN YU and TRUTHFUL under the Panama flag until broken up at Kaohsiung in 1979.

WHANGAROA
John Brown and Co. (Clydebank) Ltd., Clydebank; 1955, 8701gt, 472 feet

Like her sister, WHANGAROA was transferred to the Union company in early middle age, becoming WAINUI in 1965. A lengthy industrial dispute brought to an end her service between New Zealand and India in 1970, and she was transferred to British India as WARINA. But a year later she was hoisting a flag of convenience as the Cypriot-flag GAROUFALIA, later spending a few months as the Greek DROMEUS, before reverting to GAROUFALIA. When broken up at Kaohsiung in 1974 she was only 19 years old.

WHARANUI
John Brown and Co. (Clydebank) Ltd., Clydebank; 1956, 8701gt, 472 feet

WHARANUI is seen in the Federal colours she received in 1966. She ended her British career in British India ownership, being transferred in 1969 and renamed WAIPARA. Guan Guan (Shipping) Pte. of Singapore added her to their collection of redundant British cargo liners in 1971 and ran her as GOLDEN LION mainly between Singapore and Australia until 1979, when she made her final voyage to Kaohsiung.

TURAKINA (4)
Bartram and Sons Ltd., Sunderland; 1960, 7707gt, 455 feet

TURAKINA had some similarities to the WHAKATANE class, but had one less hold. She was built as the New Zealand company's contribution to the operations of Crusader Shipping Co. Ltd. Pictured at Auckland (top), she has the plain yellow funnel with which she was delivered, but the lower photo shows her in Crusader colours. Almost wholly refrigerated, she was built for the New Zealand to Japan service, although in her later days under P. & O. colours she traded more widely. She was sold in 1977 to the U.S.-based Uiterwyk Corporation and registered in Panama as PATRICIA U. Later names under Greek and Maltese ownership were GULF REEFER and SINES. She was broken up in mainland China in 1986. *[Top: Malcolm Cranfield]*

OTAIO (2) *(top and centre)* **and EASTERN ACADEMY** *(bottom)*
John Brown and Co. (Clydebank) Ltd., Clydebank; 1958, 13314gt, 526 feet

OTAIO was the last in the company's honourable line of dedicated training ships, carrying 40 deck cadets and - very unusually - 30 engineering cadets, who were usually trained on shore. She was basically an OTAKI class, but with the foremast moved forward and a long bridge deck to provide the necessary accommodation, classrooms, laboratories and workshops. She was described as a floating school, and besides dedicated teachers she also carried a physical training instructor. When P. & O., by then her official owners, sold her in 1976 she continued in her educational role, but this time for Gulf Shipping Lines Ltd. under the Liberian flag. Seen in the bottom photograph during April 1979 as EASTERN ACADEMY, the state of her hull would suggest that chipping and painting were not on the cadets' syllabus. After a brief period under Saudi ownership, she was broken up at Gadani Beach in 1982.

PIAKO (3)
Alexander Stephen and Sons Ltd., Linthouse; 1962, 9986gt, 488 feet

PIAKO and SOMERSET can be considered developments of the CORNWALLs, with capacity for both refrigerated and general cargo but with accommodation now trunked around the fourth hatch, as with the OTAKIs. Machinery was simplified with only one eight-cylinder Sulzer diesel, but even so PIAKO worked up to over 18 knots on trials, and could readily maintain a service speed of 16 knots. She was the last of over 20 ships, including two others of the same name, built for the group at Linthouse. With her many kingposts she had a rather old-fashioned appearance, but what looked like a derrick at the fore end of the second hatch was in fact a high speed crane of the Velle Shipshape type: the first use of one on a British ship.

PIAKO is seen in the upper photo arriving at Brisbane on her maiden voyage in March 1962, and on the Mersey in P. & O. colours during June 1975 in the lower shot. She remained under the British flag until 1979, when she went Greek as REEFER QUEEN. She was broken up at Shanghai during 1984.

SOMERSET (4)

John Brown and Co. (Clydebank) Ltd., Clydebank; 1962, 10027gt, 488 feet

Mercifully, former New Zealand and Federal ships retained their names when new owners P. & O. called their other cargo liners STRATHs in the mid-1970s. SOMERSET therefore kept her identity, along with her sister, until 1979. The top photograph shows her at Portishead in September 1971, whilst the lower one at Cardiff in October 1976 illustrates the effect of the corn-coloured hull which P. & O. inherited from Orient Line, and used rather unsuccessfully on their freighters.

As the Greek-owned and registered AEGEAN SKY she lasted until 1984 when broken up at Chittagong.

[Top: Malcolm Cranfield]

TANKERS

LINCOLN
John Brown and Co. (Clydebank) Ltd., Clydebank; 1958, 12780gt, 558 feet

In the late 1950s British companies woke up to the profitable opportunities offered by tankers. Unfortunately, many of those ordered were small by world standards, and soon became uneconomic under the British flag, as was the case with Federal's LINCOLN. After a period in Trident colours, LINCOLN was sold to the Greek Lyras group in 1965, and became the AMPHION. Phillips Petroleum bought her in 1971 and she became PHILLIPS NEW JERSEY. In 1978 she was broken up, unusually, at Brownsville, Texas.

QUILOA
Scott's Shipbuilding and Engineering Co. Ltd., Greenock; 1960, 12779gt, 560 feet

Ownership of the 17 tankers ordered by P. & O. in the late 1950s was scattered around the group's companies. QUILOA was owned by the New Zealand company, but managed by British India S.N. Co. Ltd., who provided the crew and the paint scheme. She was sold in 1972, becoming the Cypriot MICHIEL and the Panama flag GREAT JUSTICE before being broken up at Kaohsiung in 1977.

[World Ship Society collection]

DERBY
John Brown and Co. (Clydebank) Ltd., Clydebank; 1960, 31791gt, 759 feet

Like that of many British owners, Federal's involvement with tankers was ill-timed. Tanker sizes were increasing so rapidly that 30,000 tonners like DERBY quickly became outdated. Sold in 1968, she became the Liberian OKEANIS. But even the Greeks could not make a living from medium-sized turbine tankers, and OKEANIS was broken up in China during 1976.

[Fotoflite incorporating Skyfotos]

KENT (3)
John Brown and Co. (Clydebank) Ltd., Clydebank; 1960, 31763gt, 759 feet

Like her sister DERBY, KENT was sold after just eight years, and then ran under the Liberian flag as LESLIE CONWAY and then OSWEGO MERCHANT. Only sixteen years old, she was demolished at Kaohsiung in 1976.

[Fotoflite incorporating Skyfotos]

TRAMPS

KOHINUR
Charles Connell and Co. Ltd., Glasgow; 1963, 10039gt, 508 feet

In 1963 the New Zealand company took delivery of three broadly similar motor vessels which could best be described as tramps, although they spent periods on charter: KOHINUR is seen in Hamburg-Südamerikanische D.G. colours in June 1971. P. & O.'s urge for corporate identity saw her become STRATHNAIRN in 1975, but two years later she was sold to Singapore as SILVERGATE and later ANTILLA, not being broken up at Kaohsiung until 1986.

NURJEHAN
Lithgows Ltd., Port Glasgow; 1963, 8604gt, 482 feet

Both KOHINUR and NURJEHAN were originally ordered for the Asiatic Steam Navigation Co. Ltd., and retained that company's names when delivered to the New Zealand company. To make life even more confusing Hain-Nourse Ltd., the tramping arm of P. & O., were soon appointed managers. NURJEHAN spent several years on charter to Harrison Line as ADVOCATE,

and later became STRATHNEVIS. Sold to Greece in 1977 she ran as IOANNIS and DIMITRIOS P. PAPASTRATIS until broken up in India during 1984.

TRENEGLOS
William Hamilton and Co. Ltd., Port Glasgow; 1963, 9854gt, 505 feet

The motorship TRENEGLOS was ordered on behalf of the Hain Steamship Co. Ltd. but delivered to New Zealand ownership. However, for most of her life as TRENEGLOS she was under Hain or Hain-Nourse management. She became STRATHTRUIM in 1974, and names and flags subsequent to her sale in 1978 were SIAM BAY (Singapore), FAMILY ANGEL (Greek) and DOMAN (Panama). She arrived for breaking up in mainland China during August 1985.

TAUPO
Bartram and Sons Ltd., Sunderland; 1966, 10983gt, 528 feet

This group of four reefers brought the first real innovation in cargo liner design to the fleet for over 30 years. They were the first British ships to have a complete outfit of Hallen derricks, which had joystick control and could each be operated by one man. The distinctive frames at the top of the bipod masts helped to stabilise the boom by spreading the slewing guys vertically.

TAUPO remained in the P. & O. group for a number of years, eventually being officially owned by Strick Line Ltd., but without change of name and carrying P. & O.'s funnel. With this came black hulls, and then Orient Line's corn-coloured hulls, which suited these ships quite well. In June 1980 she was sold to Vestey's Singapore subsidiary Austasia Line (Private) Ltd. to become MANDAMA, and lasted as this for four years until broken up at Chittagong.

TEKOA (3)
Bartram and Sons Ltd., Sunderland; 1966, 10975gt, 528 feet

British crews did not always respect the New Zealand company's names, and TEKOA was sometimes rendered as "tea cosy". Neither were the crews impressed by the official title for the new hull colour introduced with this class, so "eau-de-nil" became "seasick green".

Give or take a few months, TEKOA's career closely paralleled that of TAUPO. Austasia called her MAHSURI, and when her turn came for the breakers it was to Kaohsiung she sailed in 1984.

TONGARIRO (4)
Bartram and Sons Ltd., Sunderland; 1966, 8233gt, 528 feet

Ownership of this group of ships was somewhat complex. Delivered to New Zealand Shipping Co. Ltd., the three Ts wore Federal funnels but flew the New Zealand company's houseflag. When Federal became official owners in 1969, the New Zealand company became managers; but all eventually were registered in the ownership of P. & O. Steam Navigation Co.

When sold in 1979 TONGARIRO joined the former PIAKO in the ownership of Theodoros Arventakis as REEFER PRINCESS. In 1982 other Greeks took her as CAPETAN LEONIDAS. Like her three less than ugly sisters she was broken up in 1985, meeting her end on Gadani Beach.

WESTMORLAND (2)
Lithgows Ltd., Port Glasgow; 1966, 11011gt, 528 feet

WESTMORLAND was the only member of this group of single-screw motorships to carry a Federal name; one which had been used before but was now spelt correctly, with only one E. WESTMORLAND was actually the first of the class to be delivered: an early application of computer-aided design led to her being completed in under eleven months.

Sold along with her sisters in 1980, WESTMORLAND became the Lebanese FARES REEFER. Unusually, in 1981 she returned to British control, becoming the Hong Kong-registered BEACON HILL owned by Dunston Shipping Co. Ltd. and managed by Blue Star. Her call to the breakers came in 1985, and she was demolished in mainland China.

MANAPOURI
Mitsui Zosen, Tamano; 1968, 9505gt, 540 feet

The year 1968 saw not only the end of the company's passenger sailings, but also the arrival of its last true cargo liners. Perhaps even more shocking was the decision to build these two freighters in Japan: the first orders placed overseas since Federal went to a French yard before the first world war. Although described as developments of the WESTMORLAND class, the distinctive appearance of the company's ships had gone and these three-quarters aft freighters could have belonged to anyone.

MANAPOURI became WILD MARLIN in 1977, and in 1982 was sold to the Comninos Brothers of Greece who named her MARATHON REEFER. In 1987 she became CORFU REEFER, and in 1990 LIMON TRADER.

MATAURA (3) *(top and centre)* **and WILD MALLARD** *(bottom)*

Mitsui Zosen, Tamano; 1968, 9504gt, 540 feet

In 1977 it was decided to include these two large and fast reefers in the Lauritzen Peninsular Reefers pool and they were renamed appropriately; MATAURA becoming WILD MALLARD. This meant the ships began life in Federal colours (top photograph), lost them for P.&O. funnels (centre), and then on renaming adopted Lauritzen or other colours. For instance, in the bottom photo taken from Penarth Head the WILD MALLARD has a rather anonymous blue funnel. She too joined the Comninos fleet in 1981, becoming MACEDONIAN REEFER, MARACAIBO REEFER in 1987 and BOLERO REEFER in 1990.

WILD AUK

A/S Bergens M/V, Bergen; 1971, 9601gt, 511 feet.

Late in 1971 P. & O. entered a joint venture with Lauritzen of Denmark under the title Lauritzen Peninsular Reefers Ltd. Both partners made a substantial investment in refrigerated ships for the pool, the first British contribution being WILD AUK which had been ordered earlier to a standard design. Towards the end of the decade, a slump in the reefer trades made the business less profitable. P. & O.'s reefers were sold and the partnership ended. WILD AUK went to Comninos Brothers in 1980 and was placed under the Greek flag as OLYMPIAN REEFER, becoming BUENOS AIRES in 1989 and the Panamanian AMAZON REEFER in 1995.

WILD AVOCET

A/S Bergens M/V, Bergen; 1972, 9710gt, 511 feet

WILD AVOCET is seen off Auckland in March 1973. By 1975, she was reported to have lost her Federal funnel colours in favour of those of P. & O. She too went to Comninos Brothers in 1980 and was renamed DELPHIC REEFER, becoming AEGEAN REEFER in 1991. *[V.H. Young and L.A. Sawyer]*

WILD CORMORANT
Lübecker Flender-Werke A.G., Lübeck; 1973, 7594gt, 507 feet.

P. & O. soon ordered further WILD reefers, this time from Germany but again to a standard design that was found in several fleets. The first was WILD CORMORANT, seen here in September 1973. In 1981 she became Comninos's ATTIKA REEFER, but changes of mind and charters have meant that subsequent names have included SILVER REEFER, BASSRO NORDIC, HORNCLIFF and TUSCAN STAR. By mid-1995 she was carrying the name FLAMINGO REEFER for the third time.

WILD CURLEW
Lübecker Flender-Werke A.G., Lübeck; 1973, 7594gt, 507 feet.

Probably because of their previous involvement with refrigerated cargo liners, Federal Steam Navigation Co. Ltd. were the registered owners of the WILD reefers. This group represented the last use of the Federal funnel, bearing the time-honoured flag with its Paget's patch. However, corporate identity reasserted itself, and the P. & O. funnel was eventually applied. WILD CURLEW's subsequent career followed that of her sister, to the extent of having sister names: ATHENIAN REEFER in 1981, GOLDEN REEFER in 1985, BASSRO ARCTIC in 1988, CARIOCAS REEFER in 1988, 1990 and 1992, HORNSEA in 1990 and CAP CORRIENTES in 1990.

WILD FLAMINGO
Drammen Slip & Verksted, Drammen; 1973, 6925gt, 474 feet

The last new ships delivered in Federal colours were the first two of a quartet of reefers from Norway for the Lauritzen Peninsular pool. Capable of 23 knots, they were again to their builder's standard design and were notable for their long forecastles.

Seen here in March 1975, WILD FLAMINGO was sold in 1983 to become the Singapore-flag REEFER CIKU. In 1987 she went to Cyprus owners and was renamed FRIO CHILE, although from 1993 to 1994 she carried the name LAS PALMAS. But it was as FRIO CHILE that on 4th January 1995 she began taking in water whilst on a voyage from Callao to Japan with a cargo of frozen squid. She sank four days later with the loss of two of her crew.

WILD REEFERS (continued)

WILD FULMAR
Drammen Slip & Verksted, Drammen; 1974, 6925gt, 474 feet

The final four WILD reefers were sold en bloc to Singapore's Sembawang Reefer Lines, and continued operating alongside the Lauritzen ships. WILD FULMAR became REEFER DUKU in 1983, STARSEA in 1988 and MIDWAY in 1990. Owned in Hong Kong, MIDWAY was damaged by fire in May 1990, and broken up in India during 1992.

WILD GANNET
Drammen Slip & Verksted, Drammen; 1977, 6933gt, 474 feet

When sold to Sembawang in 1983 WILD GANNET was given the rather unappetising name REEFER MANGGIS. In 1990 she was sold to Comninos, who were collecting former WILD reefers, and renamed IONIC REEFER.

[Fotoflite incorporating Skyfotos]

WILD GREBE
Drammen Slip & Verksted, Drammen; 1978, 6925gt, 474 feet

WILD GREBE became REEFER NANGKA in 1983. Comninos caught up with her in 1990, and she became the AEOLIC REEFER under the Greek flag.

ENTON (1)
Furness Shipbuilding Co. Ltd., Haverton Hill-on-Tees; 1925, 4425gt, 376 feet.

In 1925 Birt, Potter and Hughes Ltd., the founders of Federal, formed the Avenue Shipping Co. Ltd. to operate two early motorships, ENTON and WINTON. Seen here at Vancouver in May 1929, ENTON was fitted with a two-stroke engine of Sulzer design, built on Tyneside. She was named after the Surrey home of one of the partners.

Neither of the Avenue ships was to have a long career: ENTON was wrecked on a reef off New Caledonia on 28th January 1931 whilst on a voyage from New York to New Zealand. By coincidence, the similar-sized WINTON also came to grief just before her sixth birthday. The name chosen for the company deserves comment: was it a coincidence that their telephone exchange was called "AVEnue"?   [F.W. Hawks]

ENTON (2)
Alexander Stephen and Sons Ltd., Linthouse; 1952, 6443gt, 444 feet

Federal and New Zealand ships had occasionally been registered under the ownership of various partners and associates but were otherwise named, painted and run as part of the parent fleets. An exception was the second ENTON of 1952, which was owned by Birt, Potter and Hughes Ltd. Their funnel colours are seen in close-up in the centre photograph: red, with two blue over white pennants, and a black top. As the bottom photograph shows, ENTON was very much a Federal ship, although she had no exact sisters in that fleet. She lacked the refrigerated capacity of her contemporaries, but had a similar outfit of derricks. In 1955 she was transferred to the born-again Avenue Shipping Co. Ltd., and her further career is described on the next page.   [Middle: V.H. Young and L.A. Sawyer]

LIMERICK
Alexander Stephen and Sons Ltd., Linthouse; 1952, 6443gt, 444 feet

In 1954 the title Avenue Shipping Co. Ltd. was revived as a joint venture between Birt, Potter and Hughes Ltd. and New Zealand Shipping Co. Ltd. This was a somewhat incestuous business, as Federal were the major shareholders in Birt, Potter and Hughes Ltd. The contribution to the Avenue fleet made by Birt, Potter and Hughes Ltd. was ENTON, transferred in 1955 and renamed LIMERICK. Like the MANZ Line motorships, which were transferred to Avenue ownership at the same time, management of LIMERICK was placed in the hands of Trinder, Anderson and Co. Ltd.

Avenue operated mainly between Europe and Australia and New Zealand, more or less in parallel with the Federal and New Zealand ships but carrying cargoes that did not need refrigeration. LIMERICK ran on these services until 1969, when she was transferred within the P. & O. group to become British India's HOWRA. Three years later she was sold to Guan Guan Shipping (Pte.) Ltd. of Singapore, and as GOLDEN HAVEN her Doxford engine drove her on until she reached the breakers at Karachi in 1982.

DONEGAL
Alexander Stephen and Sons Ltd., Linthouse; 1957, 6327gt, 460 feet

The ships delivered to Avenue had grey hulls, although retaining other Federal features such as the white line separating the boot topping. The motorship DONEGAL was to see out the Avenue's independent existence, and in 1972 was registered in the ownership of P. & O., although adoption of the corporate name STRATHIRVINE did not occur for over three years. In 1977 she was sold to a group based in the Maldives, which placed her under the Panama flag. She ran as ATHINA for three years, being broken up at Kaohsiung in 1980.

GALWAY
Smith's Dock Co. Ltd., Middlesbrough; 1959, 6409/9539gt, 469/525 feet

Not surprisingly, Avenue ships had more than a family resemblance to Federal colours and nomenclature, having an "A" on a diamond at the centre of the flag, and carrying the names of Irish rather than English counties: a practice which had been applied to some Houlder ships acquired back in 1912.

GALWAY is seen following the two major events in her Avenue career. The upper photograph was taken a day after her collision with the B.P. tanker CLYDE EXPLORER near Cardiff on 22nd December 1962, and shows a gaping hole in her bow. The lower photograph shows her as lengthened at her builders' North Shields yard in 1967. Her subsequent career paralleled that of her one-time sister DONEGAL: passing to P. & O. in 1972 and becoming STRATHINVER in 1975. In 1976 she was sold, going to Singapore's Guan Guan Shipping (Pte) Ltd. and becoming GOLDEN FORTUNE. However, fortune deserted her at Hong Kong in September 1983 when a typhoon drove her aground and left her fit only for scrap.

CONTAINER SHIP

REMUERA (3)
Swan Hunter Shipbuilders Ltd., Walker Shipyard, Newcastle; 1973, 42007gt, 827 feet.

Not strictly a New Zealand ship, the partially-refrigerated container carrier REMUERA is included as the last to bear a company name. She was intended to be the first of four, but changes in the frozen meat trade, and particular Britain's membership of the European Community, led to the cancellation of the others. REMUERA was built for P. & O., and initially carried their funnel, but within months of delivery was chartered to Associated Container Transportation (Australia) Ltd. in whose funnel she is seen here in a classic Sydney setting. On completion of this charter in 1977 she was renamed REMUERA BAY, in line with the vessels of Overseas Containers Ltd., which were subsequently integrated into the P. & O. fleet.

Originally turbine-driven, she was converted to a motorship in 1983. Major fuel savings were expected from this change, especially at the speeds needed to maintain her schedule of 70-day round trips between Europe, Australia and New Zealand. When this is compared with the relatively leisurely schedule of the cargo passenger liners, which managed perhaps two round trips each year, it can be understood why the attractive ships in this book have been largely replaced with vessels as unappealing as REMUERA.

[V.H. Young and L.A. Sawyer]

INDEX
Names in capitals are those carried by ships in photographs

Back cover, upper:
HORORATA (2); *early morning at Wellington Harbour (see page 41)*
[V.H. Young and L.A. Sawyer]

Back cover, lower:
WESTMORLAND (2) *(see page 79)*